Cross

Series editors: Ian Coffey (NT), Stephen Gaukroger (OT)
Old Testament editor: Stephen Dray
New Testament editor: Steve Motyer

Titles in this series

Galatians:
Crossway Bible Guide

Simon Jones

Crossway Books Nottingham

INTER-VARSITY PRESS
Norton Street, Nottingham NG7 3HR, England
Email: ivp@ivpbooks.com
Website: www.ivpbooks.com

First published 2007

British Library Cataloguing in Publication Data
A catalogue record for this book is available from the British Library.

ISBN: 978–1–85684–227–3

Set in Palatino
Typeset in Great Britain by Avocet Typeset, Chilton, Aylesbury, Bucks
Printed in Great Britain by Creative Print and Design (Wales),
Ebbw Vale

CONTENTS

Acknowledgments

No book is a solo venture – a Bible study guide less than most. So a few thank-yous are in order:

To the New Testament editor of this series, Steve Motyer, whose wisdom saved me from a few blunders along the way – though any remaining inaccuracies and misjudgments are entirely down to me.

Liz, my administrative assistant, who proof-read the manuscript and made numerous suggestions that immeasurably improved what I'd written.

And to the guys from the Monday evening men's Bible study who allowed me to road-test these studies on them. Thanks for your patience, fellowship and good humour, guys. This book wouldn't have been finished without you!

Simon Jones
June 2006

Welcome!

These days, meeting together to study the Bible in groups appears to be a booming leisure-time activity in many parts of the world. In the United Kingdom alone, it is estimated that over one million people each week meet in home Bible-study groups.

This series has been designed to help such groups and, in particular, those who lead them. These Bible Guides are also very suitable for individual study, and may help hard-pressed preachers, teachers and students too (see 'How to use this Bible Guide', p. 9).

We have therefore enlisted authors who are in the business of teaching the Bible to others and are doing it well. They have kept in their sights two clear aims:

1. To explain and apply the message of the Bible in non-technical language.

2. To encourage discussion, prayer and action on what the Bible teaches.

All of us engaged in the project believe that the Bible is the Word of God – given to us in order that people might discover him and his purposes for our lives. We believe that the sixty-six books which go to make up the Bible, although written by different people, in different places, at different times, through different circumstances, have a single unifying theme: that theme is Salvation. This means free forgiveness and the removal of all our guilt, it means the gift of eternal life, and it means the wholeness of purpose and joy which God has designed us to experience here and now, all of this being made possible through the Lord Jesus Christ.

How to use this Bible Guide

These guides have been prepared both for personal study and for the leaders and members of small groups. More information about group study follows on the next few pages.

You can use this book very profitably as a personal study guide. The short studies are ideal for daily reading: the first of the questions provided is usually aimed to help you with personal reflection (see 'How to tackle personal Bible study'). If you prefer to settle down to a longer period of study, you can use groups of three to five studies, and thus get a better overview of a longer Bible passage. In either case, using the Bible Guide will help you to be disciplined about regular study, a habit that countless Christians have found greatly beneficial.

Yet a third use for these Bible Guides is as a quarry for ideas for the busy Bible teacher, providing outlines and application for those giving talks or sermons or teaching children. You will need more than this book can offer, of course, but the way the Bible text is broken down, comments are offered and questions are raised may well suggest directions to follow.

How to tackle personal Bible study

We have already suggested that you might use this book as a personal study guide. Now for some more detail.

One of the best methods of Bible study is to read the text through carefully several times, possibly using different versions or translations. Having reflected on the material, it is a good discipline to write down your own thoughts before doing anything else. At this stage it can be useful to consult another background book. See 'For further reading' on page 139. If you are using this book as your main study resource, then read through the relevant sections carefully, turning up the Bible references that are mentioned. The questions at the end of each chapter are specifically designed to help you to apply the passage to your own situation. You may find it helpful to write your answers to the questions in your notes.

It is a good habit to conclude with prayer, bringing before God the things you have learned.

If this kind of in-depth study is too demanding for you and you have only a short time at your disposal, read the Bible passage, read the comments in the Bible Guide, think round one of the questions and commit what you have learned to God in a brief prayer. This would take about fifteen minutes without rushing it.

How to tackle your group Bible study

1. Getting help

If you are new to leading groups, you will obviously want to get all the help you can from ministers and experienced friends. Books are also extremely helpful and we strongly recommend a book prepared by the editors of this series of Bible Guides: *Housegroups: The Leaders' Survival Guide*, edited by Ian Coffey and Stephen Gaukroger (Crossway Books, 1996). This book looks at the whole range of different types of group, asking what is the point of it all, what makes a good leader, how to tackle your meeting, how to help the members, how to study, pray, share and worship, and plenty of other pointers, tips and guidelines.

This book is a 'must' for all leaders of small groups. It is written by a team of people widely experienced in this area. It is available at your local Christian bookshop. If you have difficulty in obtaining a copy, write to Crossway Books, Norton Street, Nottingham NG7 3HR, UK.

2. Planning a programme with your Bible Guide

This guide is a commentary on God's Word, written to help group members to get the most out of their studies. Although it is never ideal to chop up Scripture into small pieces, which its authors never intended, huge chunks are indigestible and so we have tried to provide a diet of bite-sized mouthfuls.

If you want to get an overview of the Bible book in a series of meetings, you will need to select appropriate studies for each meeting. Read them yourself first and prepare a short summary of the studies you are tackling for your group. Ideally you could write it on a sheet of A5 paper and hand a copy to each member.

If you do not intend to cover the whole Bible book, choose a series of studies to suit the number of meetings you have available. It is a good idea to use consecutive studies, not to dodge about. You will then build up a detailed picture of one section of Scripture.

3. Preparing to lead

Reading, discussing with friends, studying, praying, reflecting on life … preparation can be endless. But do not be daunted by that. If you wait to become the perfect leader you will never start at all. The really vital elements in preparation are:

▶ prayer (not only in words but an attitude of dependence on God: 'Lord, I can't manage this on my own')

▶ familiarity with the study passage (careful reading of the text, the Bible Guide study and any other resource books that throw light on it) and

▶ a clear idea of where you hope to get in the meeting (notes on your introduction, perhaps, recap what was covered at the last meeting, and what direction you hope the questions will take you in – don't force the group to give your answers).

Here is a short checklist for the busy group leader:

Have I prayed about the meeting?
What do I want to achieve through the meeting?
Have I prepared the material?
Am I clear about the questions that will encourage positive group discussion?
Am I gently encouraging silent members?
Am I, again gently, quietening the chatterers?
Am I willing to admit ignorance?
Am I willing to listen to what the group members say and to value their contributions?
Am I ready not to be dogmatic, not imposing my ideas on the group?
Have I planned how to involve the members in discovering for themselves?
Have I developed several 'prayer points' that will help focus the group?
Are we applying Scripture to our experience of real life or only using it as a peg to hang our opinions on?
Are we finding resources for action and change or just having a nice talk?
Are we all enjoying the experience together?

Finding your way around this book

In our Bible Guides we have developed special symbols to make things easier to follow. Every study therefore has an opening section which is the passage in a nutshell.

The main section is the one that *makes sense of the passage.*

Questions

Every passage also has special questions for personal and group study after the main section. Some questions are addressed to us as individuals, some speak to us as members of our church or home group, while others concern us as members of God's people worldwide. The questions are deliberately designed

▶ to get people thinking about the passage

▶ to apply the text to 'real-life' situations

▶ to encourage reflection, discussion and action!

As a group leader you may well discover additional questions that will have special relevance to your group, so look out for these and note them in your preparation time.

Digging deeper

Some passages require an extra amount of explanation, and we have put these sections into different categories. The first kind gives additional background material that helps us to understand something factual. For example, if we dig deeper into the Gospels, it helps us to know who the Pharisees were, so that we can see more easily why they related to Jesus in the way they did. These technical sections are marked with a spade.

Stop and think

This feature appears with passages which highlight important themes or teaching. Bible references and questions will help you think them through.

Has anyone got a map?

Paul wrote this short, sharp letter in a hurry to a group of churches that he had founded a few years before, in the Roman province of Galatia (modern Turkey). The people that he wrote to were predominantly Gentile converts. He was in a hurry because he was about to leave Antioch for a meeting in Jerusalem that would determine the future shape of the Christian faith.

The issue to be debated in Jerusalem is the one that caused Paul to write to his young converts – namely that some were teaching that in order to be a 'Christian' you had to become a 'Jew' by keeping the law and observing the ritual boundary markers that separated Jew from Gentile – especially circumcision for men.

Paul wrote to the churches in Galatia to defend his view that all anyone needed to do to be a Christian was to trust in Jesus. He wrote in an agitated state, angry that his converts were being troubled by what he regarded as false teaching, and angry that some of them appeared to be attracted to the teaching of his rivals.

All through this Bible Guide, I refer to the other teachers as Paul's rivals or the rival missionaries. Others refer to these people as Judaizers or false teachers, but neither is helpful since both assume, with the benefit of hindsight, that Paul was right and they were wrong.

It's crucial for us to realize that at this time the future of the church and the message about Jesus was poised on a knife-edge. There were many who passionately believed that Jesus was the Jewish Messiah, and anyone who wanted to follow him would have to become Jewish. They took their case to Jerusalem as Luke tells us in Acts 15.

Others believed that the good news was for the whole world as had always been God's intention and he was redefining his holy people in relation to Jesus. This was

Paul's view and it was the view that prevailed at the Jerusalem meeting.

It is this that makes Galatians such an exciting and crucial letter. It is about nothing less than who are the people of God and how they should live in the world both as individuals and more importantly as a community of believers. It's about the freedom we can experience in Jesus – freedom from sin and religion, freedom to live lives of joyful service.

So, let's buckle up and get ready for the ride of a lifetime!

North and south – does geography matter?

Paul visited Galatia twice – on his first and again on his second missionary journeys. There is some debate about which group of churches he wrote to. If his recipients are in northern Galatia, then the letter went to churches he planted on the first stage of his second missionary journey recorded in Acts 16, some time in the early to mid 50s. If his original hearers lived in southern Galatia, then they were part of a group of churches planted on Paul's missionary journey in the mid to late 40s and detailed in Acts 13 – 14. The destination of the letter has a vital bearing on the date of it and, crucially, on whether it was written before or after the Jerusalem meeting that Luke tells us about in Acts 15.

My view is that Galatians was written in 48–49 to the churches of south Galatia as Paul was preparing to leave for the Jerusalem meeting. For reasons I explain in the 'Digging deeper' section on Paul's conversion and life story (see p. 29), I think that dating Galatians before the Jerusalem meeting makes harmonizing Paul's account of his life and Luke's record in Acts more straightforward.

It also helps to account for Paul's hurried writing style and the fact that he makes no reference at all to the apostolic decree reported in Acts 15:23–29. If he were writing after the Jerusalem meeting, quoting what James said would have sunk the argument of the rival missionaries. Paul's silence about it can mean only one of three things: either he wrote Galatians before the Jerusalem meeting; Paul didn't like the outcome so makes no mention of it (but since he 'won' at the meeting, that seems unlikely); or Luke has invented the meeting to suit his theological purposes (this too is unlikely given Luke's care to get his history right).

One other reason favouring a south Galatian destination and early date for the letter is the reference to Barnabas in Galatians 2:9 and 13. Paul doesn't explain who he is; he wouldn't need to if he was writing to churches planted on the first missionary journey when Barnabas was his colleague. If he'd been writing to churches in the north of the province, however, he would have had to explain who Barnabas was, as by that stage he was no longer part of Paul's team.

These questions, while interesting and important in creating as accurate a picture of the history of early Christianity as we can, do not affect the central message of Galatians. Paul writes to defend his gospel of law-free, Spirit-led Christianity that remains vital and vibrant for every generation of readers whether first-century Galatia or twenty-first-century anywhere on earth.

Routes through Galatians

1. The community of faith

The essentials: 2:15–16
Focused on Jesus: 2:17–21
Fulfilling the law: 3:10–14
One family: 3:26–29
Worship in the Spirit: 4:1–11
Looking out for each other: 6:1–5

2. Paul the model pastor

Preaching the truth regardless: 1:11–24
Opposing error: 2:11–14
Showing his heart: 4:12–20
A passion for essentials: 6:11–18

3. Life in the Spirit

Faith and the Spirit: 3:1–5
The Spirit and the promise: 3:10–14
The Spirit of sonship: 4:1–11
The fruits of the Spirit: 5:22–26
The Spirit and mutual care: 6:1–5

4. Reading the Old Testament as Christians

Digging deeper: Paul's use of the Old Testament (p. 67)
Christians and Abraham's story: 3:1–9
The promise fulfilled: 3:10–14
Applying the story to our lives: 4:21–31
Fulfilling the heart of the law: 5:13–15

5. Who are the people of God?

Those with faith: 2:15–16
The seed of Abraham: 3:15–18
The promised single family: 3:26–29
Those set free to serve: 5:13–15
Those who care for each other: 6:1–5
A fulfilled Israel: 6:11–18

6. How do I live as a Christian?

Dying with Christ: 2:17–21
Putting my trust in God: 3:1–9
Set free by Jesus: 5:1–6
Serving God in the church and the world: 5:13–15
Walking in the Spirit: 5:22–26
Mutual love and care: 6:1–10
(see also the 'Stop and think' section on our identity in Christ, p. 132)

FREEDOM AND MY STORY

Galatians 1 – 2

1:1–5

Getting the niceties over

Paul's in a hurry to cut to the chase. His greetings here are terse but tinged with hints of what's to come.

Not for the Galatians a reminiscence about their first meeting, a report of what Paul's been praying about or even a résumé of his travel plans. No. In one of the shortest introductory sections of any of his letters, Paul says who he is and who's sent him before launching into a withering attack on his readers' progress. But the little he says by way of introduction reveals a huge amount about himself, his faith and the heart of the issue he'll be dealing with in the rest of the letter.

Paul reminds his hearers what he is and what he isn't. He isn't the lackey of some group, sent with the authority of a human institution, carrying letters of commendation or certificates listing his qualifications. This becomes crucial later in the chapter – he isn't Jerusalem's man (1:11–12, 16, 19) – and he states it at the outset in no uncertain terms (1). Rather, he has been directly commissioned and sent by God with a message he's received by revelation (1:12b). He is an apostle (1), an appointed and anointed messenger of the King who has been sent to bring about the obedience of the Gentiles (Romans 1:5).

Uniquely in Galatians, Paul stresses that there are lots of people with him as he writes, that they are, in a sense, co-senders of the letter (2). The Greek here is 'brothers' (*adelphoi*) which might mean a close group of fellow-workers but is more likely to mean all the Christians around him at the time of writing and so include women as well as men.

He does this for two reasons. First, he wants to emphasize that the view of the gospel he's about to defend is not unusual. Rather, it's commonly held. He's probably writing from Antioch, his sending church, at the end of the 40s, in the period immediately before the meeting in Jerusalem described in Acts 15. All the believers in Antioch are united behind Paul's gospel – which is also the gospel preached by Barnabas (Acts 11:19–26, especially 26).

Secondly, Paul is going to stress that he received his message by revelation, rather than from other Christian leaders, in order to reinforce his claim that what he says is true – regardless of what others might say, even if those 'others' claim the authority of the leaders of the church in Jerusalem. But this does not mean that he is an isolated maverick. Far from it. He has planted and built a number of churches by proclaiming this message he received, a message which is bearing fruit everywhere it's preached precisely because it is the truth (Colossians 1:5b–6). All the people who are with him are evidence of this.

But the thrust of these opening verses has to do with the message itself rather than the messenger. He has been sent by the One who raised Jesus from the dead – the powerful, all-conquering Creator God (1). It's interesting in the light of his stress on the work of the Holy Spirit later in the letter that he makes no reference to the role of the Spirit in his call or more importantly in the raising of Jesus – as he does in Romans 1:4, where he is also describing his authority to teach. Perhaps he is keen to emphasize that Jesus is the Lord he serves, the one who met him on the Damascus Road and commissioned him to take the Good News of his lordship to the Gentiles. Perhaps also he wants to focus his readers' minds on Jesus alone, because when he gets into the meat of the letter he stresses that we both enter and stay in the people of God solely through our faith in Jesus (see especially 2:15–16): Jesus *is* the message.

Having spoken of Jesus being raised, he quickly introduces the theme of the cross (4) – a theme that will dominate the letter. Note the language he uses here in talking about the crucifixion: 'who gave himself for our sins to rescue us from the present evil age'. Here Paul frames his good news in an apocalyptic understanding of the world and the purposes of God, an understanding that bookends this letter as he returns to it in 6:14–16. (The clue here is that Paul speaks of the present evil age, a term derived from apocalyptic thinking; see 'Stop and think', p. 38.)

Paul asserts that we live in an age controlled by malign forces which lie behind false ideas, half-truths, traditions that enslave people, customs and practices that rob us of our freedom (see 4:3–9; Colossians 2:8; Ephesians 2:1–3). He is laying the foundation for his attack on those who are telling the Galatian Christians that they must observe the works of the law if their salvation is to be secure (see 'Stop and think', p. 81). Such teaching belongs to the present evil age from which Jesus' death and resurrection has rescued us. The followers of God's Messiah live in the age to come, an age marked by freedom, life, peace, joy and grace – hence his greeting (3).

But his language about the cross also emphasizes the grace of our Lord Jesus: he *gave* himself. The Son of God, the fulfilment of God's dealings with sinful people, the one born in the fullness of time and at the right time (4:4–5), came willingly to die for the sins of the world. It is another theme that permeates the letter and especially Paul's grasp of the personal nature of the sacrifice of Jesus (see 2:19–20; 6:14). It is that grace Paul wants his readers to experience afresh (3) as they feed on the meat of this letter. For, as they reorient their lives around the teaching Paul lays out here, they will know again the peace that comes from God the Father and our Lord Jesus Christ (3).

Questions

1. Paul was sure of his calling and identity as a Christian. How do we describe ourselves to one another? And to those we live next door to? Work with?
2. Where do we see the evidence that we live in 'the present evil age'?

3. What do these verses tell us about Jesus Christ?
4. How does being part of a church help us to know the truth of what we believe?

Making sense of Galatians

A number of times in this guide, I'll make reference to what the Greek says, as this can often enhance our understanding of Galatians.

The New Testament was written in Greek. Indeed, it is a form of Greek known as *koine* (the Greek word for 'common'), because it was the language of the streets and the marketplace rather the language of great Greek literature.

All translators have to choose between a number of options when they pick a word in English with which to translate a word from the Greek. These choices can reflect slightly different emphases. In order for every reader to get the best out of the New Testament, I recommend a number of simple strategies:

▶ Use at least two translations regularly. The best English translations for regular use are the New International Version and the New Revised Standard Version.

▶ Get a study Bible. There are good ones for both the NIV and NRSV. A study Bible has detailed notes at the foot of each page explaining difficult parts of the text, often telling readers why the translators chose certain words in preference to others, as well as providing cross-references to other parts of Scripture.

▶ Have a commentary on each book of the New Testament that refers to the Greek text, so that we don't miss anything that could be enlightening.

▶ Learn Greek. It's not as fanciful as it sounds. After all, many people learn languages to enhance their enjoyment of opera or classic Greek poetry, or simply to get more out of overseas holidays. Look out for an Interlinear New Testament to help you.

We can trust the translations of the Bible that we use. They are based on the best and most careful scholarship. There are just the odd moments where translators have to make a judgment call that will not be shared by all commentators. These probably apply to less than five per cent of the New Testament.

1:6–10

The message of freedom

The good news of Jesus sets us free – but only if we don't live our lives looking over our shoulders wondering what those around us think.

You can almost feel Paul trembling with indignation as he launches into his rebuke of the Galatian Christians. Having reminded them of the heart of the Christian message in his terse introduction, he expresses astonishment (6) that these believers should be straying from it. Later he will suggest they've been bewitched (3:1), so amazing is it that they have wandered from the simple truth of the gospel.

Paul's words tumble out as though his mind is racing faster than his lips' ability to form the sounds his secretary is committing to parchment. He curses those who preach a different gospel and he pits himself against any who would do Christian work in order to gain the favour of people. It's strong stuff. But what exactly is Paul's complaint?

He establishes two key points in this section, both of which have a bearing on our freedom. The first is that there is only one gospel. The second is that the only approval that matters is God's and that true freedom flows from following his call.

At this point Paul doesn't outline the content of the teaching that is leading the Galatian believers astray. Later he tells us that it centred on the view that followers of Jesus must keep the Jewish law. In particular, Paul is challenging the teachers, who are insisting that if we are to be part of the people of God, we must be circumcised (if we're a man), keep the Sabbath and follow the dietary regulations laid out in the Torah (see 'Stop and think', p. 81). Here it is sufficient for him to contrast this teaching with his gospel of grace (6).

He has harsh words for those who depart from the message as Paul has preached it: theirs is a 'different gospel' (6), 'confusing' (7), they 'pervert the gospel of Christ' (7), 'let that one be accursed' (8c, 9c, NRSV).

It's clear that the teachers who were contradicting Paul claimed some pretty weighty authority for their actions – probably the approval, if not the mandate, of the leaders of the church in Jerusalem, especially James, the Lord's brother. This is why Paul tells them firmly that whoever might preach it – even an angel from heaven (8) – they should not believe it.

How will they tell the true gospel from the false one? The clue is in the phrase 'the grace of Christ' (6). Paul's gospel, the true gospel, centres on the grace of Jesus revealed in his death and resurrection, as Paul has already reminded us (1, 3–4). This gospel centres on God's free gift of rescue from the present evil age, forgiveness of sins and peace with the Father (3–4). It is on this message and no other that our freedom rests.

And that freedom for Paul is crucially about freedom from religion with its never-ending duties and lists of 'do's' and 'don'ts'. The false teachers in Galatia, the rival missionaries, those who said effectively that you had to be Jewish to be a Christian (see 'Digging deeper', p. 41), were laying on the Gentile converts in these small churches a burden Paul felt was intolerable, as well as being a denial of the gospel of Christ.

One of the problems of religion is that it clutters people's lives with rules and regulations. Religion hems people in and robs them of their freedom. It also hands power over their lives to religious elites and leaders. This was Jesus' complaint against the Pharisees. It is a battle Paul constantly waged all over the Eastern Mediterranean as he sought to protect the churches he planted from the invasion of Judaizing tendencies.

Religion also tends to disturb or confuse (7), whereas the gospel of grace brings peace (3). Paul is not just engaging in a war of ideas or theories. It matters what people are taught because their lives, their well-being hangs on it. Paul's concern is that these young believers are nurtured in the true faith. Later he will liken his ministry to childbirth and himself to these believers' mother, so passionate is he that they remain on the path he has set them off on (4:19). Paul longs for his readers to know the peace that comes from the true gospel rather than the confusion sown by religion.

And this leads to the second major point Paul makes in these verses: whose approval matters to us – man's or God's? Paul's attack is against other missionaries, other church planters and ministers who are travelling in the same area as Paul, but preaching a different gospel (7). The issue his readers must face is this: are they becoming servants of God or of particular teachers (cf. 4:17)?

Paul's concern is that each of his readers grows up to be the person God has created them to be in Christ. It is the model Paul sets before them from his own life (10). The crucial question each of them faces is: will I follow Jesus into the freedom he's won for me on the cross or will I bind myself to a teacher who will fill my life with rules and regulations and rob me of that freedom? Paul knows what he would choose. He appeals to his readers to choose the same.

Questions

1. What different gospels are there in our churches today? How can we tell when they've departed from the true gospel?
2. How do we understand our freedom in Christ?
3. Is the Christian faith a 'religion'? What role does religious observance play in our faith?
4. Does Christian 'freedom' sometimes mean breaking the rules? What rules would you like to break – and why? What stops you?

Paul's conversion and life story: fitting Acts and Galatians together

We have two major sources for information about Paul's life – his letters and Luke's account of the growth of the early church in Acts. Do they tell us the same thing? Scholars disagree. Some argue that Acts is not a reliable source and that it's all-but impossible to harmonize the information Luke gives us with Paul's own accounts.

But comparing the story Paul tells of himself in Galatians with Luke's narrative in Acts, it is possible to produce a version of the story that both sources agree on. This is what we attempt here.

It's my view that Galatians was written in a hurry just before Paul departed for the major meeting of church leaders Luke tells us about in Acts 15:4–29 (see 'Has anyone got a map?' p. 15). What Paul tells us about his life up to that point in Galatians can be brought into agreement with what Luke tells us about the fiery apostle in his account, as the following table shows:

Table 1: Comparing Paul's and Luke's version of the apostle's life story

1: Galatians 1:13–14	Acts 7:58 – 8:3
2: Galatians1:15–17	Acts 9:3–5
3: Galatians 1:18–24	Acts 9:23–30; 11:25–26
4: Galatians 2:1–10	Acts 11:27–30
5: Galatians 2:11–14	Acts 15:1–2

This is a very reasonable way of reading Acts that indicates that when Paul says he's telling the truth and not lying (Galatians 1:20), we can believe him because Luke tells us the same story. It also means that we can put the two accounts together to create a clearer picture of Paul's earlier life.

Having persecuted the followers of Jesus because he was convinced they were betraying the traditions of his ancestors (line 1 in the table), Paul met Jesus on the road to Damascus (Acts 9:1–9). Paul does not tell us about these events in detail, but, from what Luke records, we can't fail to agree with Paul's description of it: that God revealed his Son to him (line 2).

Then having spent some time in Damascus and Arabia, he came to Jerusalem (line 3). Luke expands the story for us – especially by adding the detail that Barnabas was the one who befriended the new Christian and introduced him to the other leaders (Acts 9:27). Paul doesn't mention Barnabas here (though he does in 2:11–14), perhaps because he didn't want to drag this gentle man into his fierce dispute with the Galatian Christians (except where he had no choice) and because he is at pains to stress that no human being gave him his message – not even his close colleague, Barnabas – that he received it from Jesus himself.

Luke too fleshes out Paul's reference to going to Syria and then Cilicia by telling us that he went first to his home city of Tarsus in the Roman province of Syria (Acts 9:30) and then, at Barnabas's behest, to Antioch in the province of Cilicia (Acts 11:25; line 3 of table 1).

While at Antioch, Luke tells us that prophets came from Jerusalem predicting a great famine would affect the whole of Judea. The church sent Barnabas and Paul with money for the believers there (Acts 11:27–30). This is the trip Paul tells us about in Galatians 2:1–10 (line 4 in the table). This time Paul adds the helpful detail that some fourteen years had elapsed since he first met Jesus (Galatians 2:1). At this meeting the apostles – representing the churches from the prosperous part of the Empire not hit by the famine – urged Paul to remember the poor, something Paul by his actions showed he was eager to do (Galatians 2:10; Acts 11:30).

Then Paul gives details of the events that sparked the Jerusalem meeting that Luke tells us about at great length in Acts 15. Whereas Luke merely tells us that certain people caused bother at Antioch by questioning whether Gentiles could be Christians without observing the Jewish law, Paul tells us that a fierce public row blew up involving him and Peter, a row that could only really be resolved by getting all the key church leaders together (line 5). Galatians was written in the gap between Acts 15:2a and 15:2b.

This makes sense! However, not everyone accepts this harmonization of Acts and Galatians. Some argue that because Galatians was written after the Jerusalem conference, 2:1–10 is Paul's account of it, and the incident at Antioch which he describes in 2:11–14 happened after it. This seems unlikely to me since Paul makes no reference to the outcome of the conference in his challenge to Peter, something he would have done had the conference already taken place and happened as Luke tells it.

If I am right, then the fact that Paul and Luke are in substantial agreement on these details of the apostle's early life suggests that we can trust what Luke tells us about Paul's later life, events for which he is the only witness we have.

31

1:11–24

The truth about me

**Paul tells his story in order to demonstrate the truth of his
message and show how it has changed his life and can
change the lives of his readers.**

Galatians 1:11 kicks off the longest auto-
biographical section of any of Paul's letters (it runs to 2:21). In great detail the
apostle recounts his life since he met
Jesus on the Damascus Road. Yet it tells us nothing about
his church planting exploits or his role as a teacher in
Antioch from where he is writing. Rather it focuses solely
on Paul's relationship with the church in Jerusalem and its
leaders.

Paul is at pains to point out that his message came
directly from God and not from any human source (11–12).
His message came by revelation (12b, 16a) not from human
teachers (11b, 16b). His telling of the story closely mirrors
Luke's account of it in Acts (see 'Digging deeper', p. 29),
but he strips out all the detail to ram home the key point
that it is God who has made him what he is now. And that
it is God – not following the religious demands of the rival
missionaries – who will make his readers (both then and
now) all that God intends them to be.

His readers know of his earlier life (13a) – probably
because he told them about it when he was with them,
though no doubt his opponents have brought it up as well
in an attempt to discredit him! He had started out as a militant Pharisee, zealous for the law, keen to rid the land of
Israel of all pollutants – of which the followers of Jesus were
one (13–14). Then he'd met Christ on the Damascus Road.

Note the language he uses. He doesn't speak of conver-

sion. He speaks of *call* in words that echo the call of
Jeremiah (Jeremiah 1:4–5, cf. Isaiah 49:1), a call to a mission – that of proclaiming Jesus to the Gentiles (16). And
note the sentence structure. The focus of the one long sentence covering verses 15–17 is in the second half of verse
16: Paul did not consult any human authority about his
call. Like the great Old Testament prophets, Paul was
called directly by God to a work God had prepared for
him before he was born. This is some claim!

What Paul is telling us is that he is more than a man
made in Tarsus, more than a well-educated Jew, zealous
for the traditions of his ancestors (14). He is someone who
has met the One who fulfils all those traditions and whose
death and resurrection have opened up the family of God
to any who believe in Jesus – including Gentiles, people
like his readers in Galatia.

And this is no human interpretation of recent historical
events. This is something that Paul has received by revelation. Of course, revelation needs to be processed. That
probably explains why, instead of going to Jerusalem, he
went to Arabia before returning to Damascus. Three years
of reflection, reading, praying, working out what on earth
had happened to him on the Damascus Road followed
that life-changing experience (18).

Then he went to Jerusalem. Luke tells us about it in Acts
9:26–30. He met some of the key leaders of the church –
namely Barnabas and the apostles, probably including
James and Peter – before having to leave because some of
his old friends wanted him dead. He went home to Syria
(Tarsus) before Barnabas found him and brought him to
Cilicia (Antioch, 21, cf. Acts 11:25–26). And although he
taught the believers there for more than a year, he was
unknown to the churches in the Jesus movement's heart-
land of Judea (23).

If we are to know the freedom Christ has won for us, we
need to know who we are and who made us who we are.
Paul tells his story here because he wants his experience to
serve as a model for his readers. So, what do we learn?

Notice how his former life was dominated by what he

wanted: '*I* was…' (13), '*I* advanced…' (14a), '*I* was… (14b, NRSV). His life now is the result of what God wants: God set him apart (15a), God called him (15b), God revealed his Son to him (16a). But notice too that God doesn't wipe out Paul's character when he calls him to new service. Paul was zealous and energetic as a persecutor of the church; he is equally zealous and energetic as a builder of it (cf. Philippians 3:4–12). Paul was knowledgeable about the traditions of his ancestors, more knowledgeable than most (14b), now he is able to understand those traditions in the light of the coming of Christ and powerfully to proclaim the message of how those traditions are fulfilled in Jesus (23–24). This paves the way, by implication, for Paul's key teaching later in the letter that the Galatians must not submit to those traditions which the rival missionaries are urging on them.

When he became a servant of Christ (10), Paul found his identity and calling. Being a church-planting Christian missionary who proclaimed salvation by faith in Christ alone – that's what God created Paul to be (15). At that moment he discovered perfect freedom, the freedom that comes when we find the purpose of our lives. He is desperate that his readers find that freedom and are not robbed of it by those who add anything to the simple message that was revealed to Paul on the Damascus Road.

Paul's freedom, as we'll see, even extended to being able to call himself a sinner (2:17), something a militant Pharisee couldn't believe of himself (cf. Philippians 3:6). But he was a sinner who'd met Jesus and been set free from his sin (1:4), free to live and proclaim the good news of Jesus, whose cross and resurrection had dealt with his sin. It's his life of freedom that he wants his readers to model theirs on.

Questions

1. Spend a little time – in a group with others if possible – describing the time you met Jesus.

2. Martin Luther, one of the great theologians of the Reformation, taught that God calls all of us (like Paul in verse 15) to be what we are – mothers, teachers, builders, farmers, artists, etc. Do you agree with Luther?
3. How did we come to be what we are today? Paul's life up to the time of writing Galatians had been formed by many different influences and experiences. What has shaped you? (It might be helpful to write things down.)

2:1–5

Agreeing the essentials

Paul's gospel and that of the Jerusalem leaders is the same in both content and consequences – only not everyone seems to believe it.

 Having established that his gospel came directly from God through revelation, Paul is now at pains to show that it agrees with the message preached by the Jerusalem church. More than that, he wants to deny any rumour that he and James might disagree on the essentials.

So Paul tells his readers about a second visit he made to Jerusalem. It happened fourteen years after his call to be an apostle (1a), rather than fourteen years after his first visit. This is the one Luke tells us about in Acts 11:27–30. Agabus came to Antioch and prophesied about an impending famine (the 'revelation' Paul refers to in 2a). The believers respond by dispatching Paul and Barnabas to Jerusalem with a gift.

Paul adds the information that they took Titus with them (1c). The reason for this becomes clear almost immediately: Titus is a Gentile but no one in Jerusalem insisted that he should be circumcised (3). Paul names him to stress the fact that his is a mixed team, united solely by their faith in Jesus. This lends support to Luke's portrait of the church in Antioch as a community made up of both Jews and Gentiles, and because of that the believers were called 'Christians' for the first time (Acts 11:26). It also offers an insight into the start of Titus' career – a man who became a prominent member of Paul's team in later years (see 2 Corinthians 2:12–13; 8:16–24; 12:17–18) and eventually leader of the church on Crete (Titus 1:4–5). It seems apparent that he is a convert from Antioch, one whom Paul is training in ministry by having him as a travelling companion.

Paul has a private meeting with the leading apostles (2) at which he laid out the core of his teaching (2b). But what are we to make of his phrase 'in order to make sure I was not running, or had not run, in vain' (2c, NRSV)? Surely he has stressed that his gospel was not learned from other people nor was it dependent on human approval (1:11–12, 16c–17a). What would have happened if the Jerusalem leaders had told him to amend his teaching? It's pretty clear from what he's already said, that he would have refused. So what's going on?

It's likely that verse 2c reflects the Jerusalem leaders' questions about Paul, not uncertainty on his part. And Paul is willing to be examined by them to show them – and his readers – that there is no division about the fundamentals of the gospel between him and his team based in Antioch and James and his team based in Jerusalem. As he asserts later in the chapter (2:15–16), people are saved by their faith in Jesus, whether they are Jews or Gentiles. He knew that when he laid out the content of his gospel before the pillar apostles, there'd be no raised eyebrows, no disagreement. Indeed, in verse 9 it is those apostles who offer Paul the right hand of fellowship and not vice versa – indicating that they are happy with what he said to them.

Thus, Paul is stressing two vital and linked truths: the

unity of the church and the truth of his message. In explaining to the leaders of the Jerusalem church what he is preaching (the verb in 2:2 about his proclamation is in the present tense, meaning that he told them then what he is still preaching now), he is making a public display of the unity of the two great mission movements of the church at that time, Jerusalem and Antioch.

By reporting this meeting in the way he does, he is simultaneously assuring his Galatian readers that the leaders of the Jerusalem church – the very people the false teachers are claiming as their authority – endorse Paul's gospel and no other.

Just as Paul is about to make this point, he goes off at a tangent (3–5 is a digression from his main argument in 2:1–10). Mentioning Titus (1) reminded him that James and the other leaders had not insisted that he should be circumcised (3), but also that some people had slipped into the meeting to cause trouble (4).

The language Paul uses here is a bit of a puzzle. He talks about them being 'false believers' who 'spy' not on Paul's meeting with the other apostles, but on 'the freedom we have in Christ' and their agenda is to 'enslave' them (4). It isn't clear who Paul is talking about or when this spying took place. But the likeliest interpretation is that these people are the same ones who have been causing trouble among the Galatians, and who arrived in Antioch causing mayhem (Acts 15:1). This would suggest that the false teachers Paul is attacking in this letter had associations with the Jerusalem church, though as Paul makes very clear in a moment, they did not represent its leaders.

Paul ends his digression by asserting that he didn't waver in his commitment to the truth of his gospel, not because he's bloody-minded and unteachable, but so that his first readers (and us) might always enjoy the truth of the real gospel of grace and freedom and not the false doctrine of the rival missionaries (5).

His focus is clear. He is not telling us history for the sake of it. He is outlining to his readers the nature of his gospel so that they may trust it and know the freedom and life that comes through it. His readers can rest easy, he is saying, because the gospel he preached to them is the same gospel as that preached by the leaders in Jerusalem – whatever the false teachers might claim.

Questions

1. If Paul was concerned about the unity of the church, what would he have made of the division of the church into 'denominations' today?
2. What is 'the freedom that we have in Christ Jesus'?
3. How might we lose it? And how should we resist losing it like Paul?
4. How can we best help young Christians grow in their faith and whatever ministries God has given them?

There's a new world coming

Paul's gospel makes no sense unless we understand that his theology operates in two time zones: the present age and the age to come. This way of seeing history was a central feature of a Jewish way of thinking and writing known as 'apocalyptic'.

Apocalyptic literature was hugely popular in Israel in the decades before and after the birth of Jesus. It was a mixture of fantasy material like *Lord of the Rings* and political diatribe, like Marx and Engels' *Communist Manifesto*. The ideas of the many books written in this style were debated and contested; they inspired hope among people who felt marginalized and oppressed; they informed the political programmes of various groups in first-century Israel, including the Pharisees and the Essenes.

All sorts of examples of this literature survive – the two best known are Daniel in the Old Testament and Revelation in the New. And while they vary considerably, they tend to share certain distinguishing features. For instance, many of them involve a prophet being taken up into the heavenly realm, where a guide – often an angel – interprets the meaning of events happening on earth and reveals the immediate future.

But at the heart of every apocalypse is the idea that the present age is evil, controlled by the forces of darkness (often embodied in the particular power occupying the land of Israel at the time of writing); but a new age is coming, a time when God will defeat all his enemies and usher in his kingdom of peace, justice and joy.

This was Paul's view of the world. He was schooled in it in his training as a Pharisee. It was what fired his zeal for the law that led him to persecute the church – for he believed it was necessary to purify Israel to make it ready for the coming of God's kingdom, and the church polluted the land and therefore needed to be wiped out.

Then Paul met Christ and he realized that God's kingdom had already begun to arrive through his chosen King, Jesus, the crucified, raised and exalted Son of God.

Galatians is not obviously apocalyptic: there are no reports of visions, no reference to the end of the world, stars falling from the heavens or the moon appearing blood-red. But an apocalyptic understanding of history is crucial for understanding Galatians. This letter is book-ended with apocalyptic imagery (1:4; 6:14–16), thus setting Paul's entire discussion in an apocalyptic framework. The gospel frees us from the present evil age and everything associated with it, he says (1:4) – divisions between people, for example, because of a new creation made possible by the cross (6:14–15).

Paul's understanding of the end of the old order and the coming of the new is fleshed out in four particular ways in Galatians:

▶ Religion is likened to a malign force that keeps people enslaved to its dark dominion. Paul describes the Galatians' pagan past as slavery to 'the weak and beggarly elemental spirits' (4:9, NRSV). Worse, he says that the law kept people bound to these 'elemental spirits'. All religion, Paul says, is a means by which the forces ranged against the true God keep people enslaved. In chapter 3 he points out that people who are under the law – either by birth (i.e. Jews) or by choice (Gentiles who submit to the law because of the influence of the false teachers) – are under a curse that can only be lifted by the victory of Jesus over the malign forces on the cross (3:10, 13, 22).

► The divisions of the old order – between Jew and Gentile, men and women, slave and free – are swept away among those who are in Christ (3:28). These divisions are the result of sin embodied in social and religious systems that enable the powerful to exploit the less powerful.

► The old division between those who keep the law of God and those who don't is swept away by the arrival of faith and the Spirit. In the present evil age, says Paul, the law is used to exclude people rather than as a beacon to enlighten people and draw them to God. In Christ there is a new order, based not on the law but on faith, not on the flesh – understood as the efforts of people – but on the Spirit, the agent of new life bursting from the future into the present (see 2:17–19; 3:12, 21–22; 4:21–31; 5:16–18, 22).

► The new world arrives through the cross of Christ and all people enter the new world now through their response to the cross. In 2:19–21 Paul talks about having been crucified with Christ by which he has died to the old order. And in 6:14 he speaks of boasting only about the cross by which 'the world has been crucified to me and I to the world', an event that ushers in a new creation. In other words, the cross is the decisive moment in history, the event that marks the crossing from the old to the new. Through the cross the old world order is ended and God's new world order, what Jesus called the Kingdom of God, is ushered in.

This apocalyptic framework is essential for seeing that Paul is not just arguing that the Christian faith is better than Judaism – or any other religion for that matter. Rather, he is arguing that all religions belong to the old order which is being swept away by God. In Christ we are part of the new order that has nothing to do with religion but everything to do with new creation and life in the Spirit.

What the rival missionaries taught

We have no independent record of what Paul's rivals taught in Galatia, but from what Paul says, we can produce an outline of their manifesto which would have contained the following:

1. *Every Christian male must be circumcised or they cannot enter a covenant relationship with Israel's God* (2:3–4, 12; 5:2–3, 6, 11–12; 6:12–15).
2. *Every Christian must observe the works of the law* – namely the food laws, the Sabbath, special days and seasons as well as circumcision (3:1–5, 10–12; 4:8–11; see 'Stop and think', p. 81)
3. *The law of Moses remains the only basis of Christian ethics* (3:16, 24).
4. *We are the representatives of the Jerusalem church and hence teach with their authority* (this is the reason for Paul's lengthy defence of his apostleship and relationship with the Jerusalem leaders in 1:13 – 2:10).
5. *We base our teaching on Abraham and especially Genesis 17 which tells the story of the origins of circumcision as a sign of membership of Abraham's family.* (They probably also made use of Deuteronomy 27 – 31 and Leviticus 18:5, which explains why Paul expounds these passages of Scripture as well as basing his key objection to their teaching on Genesis 15, the story of Abraham's justification by faith.)

6. *We are concerned for the purity of Abraham's ethnic descendants at a time of growing tensions in Israel.* In the 40s and 50s opposition to the Gentile domination of Israel was rising – it would explode in full-scale revolt in the mid-60s. There is a good case for suggesting that Paul's rivals were concerned to protect the Jewish Christians in Jerusalem from the charge of being pro-Roman, by insisting that all converts to the new Christian movement showed their allegiance to Israel's God by submitting to circumcision and the works of the law. This accounts for Paul's radical redefinition of God's people as those with faith in Jesus drawn from every nation (3:26–29; 6:12–16 – where Israel is understood not ethnically but as the people of God redefined in Christ).

For Paul, this added up to an unacceptable distortion of the gospel – hence his attack on it (1:6–9; 2:21; 4:9–11; 5:1). It's possible that his rivals bore Paul no ill-will. They may well have thought that they were merely filling in parts of the message Paul hadn't had the time to. But that's not how Paul saw it. He saw his rivals as preaching a false gospel derived from a defective understanding of the God revealed in Jesus:

1. The rivals' reliance on the works of the law indicates an inadequate understanding of who Jesus was and what he achieved on the cross.
2. Their stress on obeying the law reveals a lack of understanding of and trust in the Holy Spirit to ensure good order among God's people.
3. Their insistence that Gentiles be circumcised underestimates the reach of God's grace and completely misunderstands his plans for the church – that it be a community drawn from all nations united by its faith in Jesus and walking in the Spirit.
4. They fail to see that in the life and death of Jesus, the new age longed for by Jewish apocalyptic had dawned. They don't grasp that the coming of the Spirit means that God's future has crashed into the present, bringing

new life and the fulfilment of all the dreams of the Old Testament prophets.

In short, according to Paul, his rivals had an insufficient view of God and his grace, of Jesus and his work, of the Holy Spirit and his power, of the church as the fulfilment of God's plans for his people and of the gospel as the proclamation of God's future invading the present. Little wonder he said it was another gospel and expressed his amazement that his converts would swap the real thing for this pale imitation.

2:6–10

Co-operating in mission

United in their understanding of the core of the gospel, Paul and the Jerusalem leaders recognized the distinct nature of each other's mission.

Paul wants to do two things in tension with each other. On the one hand he wants to establish that his gospel is not dependent on human authorities because it came by revelation. On the other hand, he wants to say that it was endorsed by the leaders of the church in Jerusalem. This may explain why his tone in these verses appears somewhat dismissive. But, as is often the case with Paul, appearances can be deceptive.

After his digression about false believers (3–5), he returns to his report of the meeting with James and co. His language is far from flattering (especially in verse 6), but he's choosing his words carefully. The false teachers are clearly looking for followers, for people who will look up to them, who will acknowledge them as something special in the purposes of God. False teachers frequently have a false and somewhat inflated view of their own importance.

Paul stresses that God shows no partiality. This applies to Paul as much as to the Jerusalem leaders and it certainly applies to the false teachers. His point is that though people claim authority for themselves, it is actually only God who confers authority and that is generally shown by the fruits of people's ministries. His words here aren't aimed so much at the Jerusalem leaders or himself, as at the false teachers leading the Galatian believers up the garden path.

What matters to Paul is what God is doing and what God is entrusting to people. Hence the introduction of Peter at this point (7b). He needs to talk about Peter because he'll be reporting on his row with this apostle in a moment (11-14). But he also wants to draw a crucial parallel between Peter and himself rather than between James and himself. Why? Partly because the false teachers made so much of James, and Paul wants to remind them and his readers that other apostles were on the scene before James. But mainly because Peter was directly commissioned by Jesus to preach the gospel to the people of Israel (John 21:15-19).

The outcome of the meeting in Jerusalem was that Paul's ministry was recognized to be the equal of Peter's. For just as Peter had been commissioned by Jesus to preach the gospel to Jews (the circumcised, 7b), so it was acknowledged that Paul had been called to preach to Gentiles (the uncircumcised, 7a, 8c). And in case the readers miss the significance of this, Paul stresses that the same person did the calling in both cases, namely Jesus himself (8).

It wasn't just Peter (or Cephas) who saw this. The whole leadership did (James and John as well, 9a). And they recognized that the call had been given not only to Paul but also to Barnabas and by implication to any other they invited into their team (namely the Gentile Titus, lurking in the background at this point).

The language Paul uses here emphasizes that this is more than a mere human agreement. This is not the meeting of a sales force carving out regions from a map for various people to work. Rather, the agreement is the outcome of a recognition that God is at work, calling people to various ministries ('grace' 9b). The offering of the right hand of fellowship (9c) is an indication that there is no disagreement or rivalry between Antioch and Jerusalem, just the recognition that God had called them to different but complementary missions.

At this point the use of the words 'circumcision' and 'uncircumcision', though clumsy, becomes very important (7 – the NIV uses the words 'Jew' and 'Gentile' here, which is not as helpful as the NRSV's translation). The very issue the false teachers were emphasizing was that Gentiles needed to be circumcised if they were going to be part of the people of God (see 'Stop and think', p. 81). Here Paul demonstrates that as a result of this meeting circumcision isn't an issue, it's just a label.

James, Peter and John recognize that God has called Paul to preach Jesus to those who are not circumcised, the Gentiles, just as he has called them to preach to those who are. But the digression (3–5) demonstrates that the Jerusalem leaders were not expecting Paul to include circumcision in his gospel at all. They were coming to the view that would be fully and openly expressed at their next meeting – the one recorded in Acts 15 that took place after Galatians was written – that Gentiles could become part of the people of God solely through their faith in Jesus.

This means that circumcision is an irrelevance in terms of salvation and has merely become a way of talking about two groups of people – almost on par with the terms 'black' and 'white' in our world. This, of course, is the opposite of what the false teachers were saying.

Apart from faith in Jesus, only one thing was mentioned as being essential to the two missions: remembering the poor (10). Paul and his team had come to Jerusalem with a gift for the Judean Christians from their Gentile brothers and sisters in Antioch precisely because Paul was keen to remember the poor (Acts 11:27–30). Later in his ministry he would gather a great collection from all the Gentile churches to take to Jerusalem as a sign of the unity of Jew and Gentile in the church of Jesus Christ.

The gospels of Antioch and of Jerusalem were the same not only in content – membership of God's people came by faith in Jesus and nothing else – but also in consequence: that the poor were remembered and helped, that there was true community and sharing at an economic level among those who called on the name of Jesus. Remembering the poor – regardless of ethnicity – becomes a test of the truth of the gospel that Paul is defending in Galatians: faith in Jesus alone means we are part of one family under God, responsible for one another's well-being – both spiritual and material.

Questions

1. Are there any issues which threaten to divide your church? How can they be helpfully dealt with?
2. How do we show in practice that God doesn't make divisions between people, but accepts all equally?
3. At the same time, how can we recognize and honour the ministries of others even when they are different from ours?
4. And what about 'remembering the poor' in our churches and world today? How can we do this in a way which grows out of the gospel of our Lord Jesus Christ?

When friends fall out

This is not an argument about table manners. Paul feels that Peter's action threatens the very integrity of the gospel.

The Galatians must have heard this story before – from the false teachers, those claiming the authority of James for their corruption of the good news. Their version probably went something like this: Peter, influenced by Paul, had not observed the dietary laws when he came to Antioch until the people from James arrived and showed him his error. When that happened, Paul got angry and wrongly insisted that the law didn't matter any more and Jews and Gentiles could eat freely together.

Paul's indignation in this short section is tangible – indignation partly at being misrepresented by his opponents but mainly because those opponents were using Peter's error to back up a message that would bind this young church into a life-sapping legalism. He's horrified at the prospect!

So, let's get the story clear. Having returned from Jerusalem to Antioch, Paul was later joined by Peter. We gather from Peter's letters and subsequent church tradition that he travelled quite extensively – unlike James who seemed to stay put in Jerusalem. Paul suggests that he welcomed him as a fellow preacher and leader, and the two worked together in the various house churches in Antioch. This is the strong implication of verse 12: Peter enjoyed fellowship at mixed tables – comprising both Jewish and Gentile Christians – at which teaching and even evangelism, as well as eating, would have happened.

Everything was fine until other people came 'from

James' (verse 12). Is Paul saying that these people came with James' authority? Is he suggesting that the Jerusalem leadership sent them to check up again on what was going on in Antioch (see Acts 11:22)? This doesn't seem likely, given what Paul has already told us about his meetings in Jerusalem – especially 2:1–10. It is more likely that the group that turned up is a vocal, conservative, Jewish-Christian minority group intent on making life uncomfortable for those who enjoy the freedom of Paul's gospel: the same group that had spied on the apostles in their previous meeting (2:4–5); possibly the same group that was spreading its nonsense among the Galatians as Paul wrote these words.

If this is the case, why did Peter react the way he did? Why did he stop eating with uncircumcised Gentiles? Paul describes his behaviour as 'hypocrisy' (13, twice) by which he 'stood self-condemned' (11, NRSV). Peter had already got into trouble for eating with Gentiles (Acts 11:3), so he might have felt particularly sensitive about the issue. However, he had defended himself against criticism on that occasion by pointing out that God had poured out his Spirit on Gentiles. And in view of the meeting in Jerusalem that Paul has just reported on, it is extraordinary that Peter didn't see the implications of both the apostles' agreement there – to which he had been party – and of his actions here.

The issue for these conservative Jewish believers was simple: Jews do not eat with Gentiles, so unless the Gentile converts to Christianity are observing the strict Jewish food laws, Peter shouldn't be eating with them. But Paul assumed the 'right hand of fellowship' (9) offered in Jerusalem meant that Gentile converts didn't have to observe such works of the law (see 'Stop and think', p. 81). After all, no one had suggested that the Gentile Titus should be circumcised (2:3).

But maybe Peter had doubts. Or at least, he was uncertain enough of his ground so that when challenged by loud voices claiming the authority of James for their words, he suffered a moment of profound doubt: he doubted his new identity as a Christian and fell back into his old identity as a Jew. More than that, he seemed to be putting the opinions of others above his understanding of the gospel (see 'Stop and think', *Our identity in Christ* p. 132). The problem with this was the terrible effect that it had on other believers.

Notice that Paul says it was the Jewish Christians at Antioch who were unsettled by this, rather than the Gentile converts (13a). Even Barnabas was 'led astray'. It should be noted that Paul doesn't suggest that he and Barnabas fell out over this. Perhaps the Gentiles were a bit nonplussed by the row, a spat between Jewish believers over some arcane point of Jewish law. But it's Jewish Christians who are thrown into confusion by it. And Paul sees the danger for all concerned and felt it necessary to rebuke Peter in public (11, 14).

The issue as far as Paul is concerned is threefold. First, Peter is a leader and hence an example. His behaviour influenced people, clearly seen in the effect Peter's action had on even a mature Christian like Barnabas (13). So he needs to be consistent. If he believes it's okay to eat with Gentile converts in Antioch, then he must be prepared to eat with them whoever else is in the room. Peter is behaving like the Christian who drinks alcohol with those brothers and sisters who also drink alcohol, but who condemns alcohol among teetotallers. This is hypocrisy, 'not acting consistently with the truth of the gospel' (14, NRSV).

Secondly, such inconsistency can lead to questions being raised about the truth of the gospel. Peter wasn't guilty of false teaching but of false living that sowed confusion among the believers. Paul has been establishing that the gospel sets us free – free from sin, from religion, from the opinions of others. The trouble with Peter's action is not just that he behaved inconsistently, but that his act of withdrawing from the Gentiles when the Jerusalem people arrived created confusion in the minds of those Gentiles over what was proper Christian conduct. Peter seemed more concerned to protect his reputation in the eyes of the conservative newcomers than to live consistently with his principles derived from the gospel and his experience of God's grace shown to Jew and Gentile equally (see the story of Cornelius in Acts 10:1–11, 18). It's a danger we all face – however far advanced we are in the Christian faith.

Thirdly, Peter's denial of the freedom we enjoy in Christ destroyed the unity between Jewish and Gentile believers and hence was a denial of the very gospel itself. The key here is verse 14. These old distinctions between Jew and Gentile are irrelevant! Christ has freed us from the present evil age where such distinctions matter (1:4). Indeed, in Christ, there are no such distinctions (3:28), because a new world has come where we are free to eat and share fellowship with all who own the name of Jesus regardless of their ethnicity, gender or social class.

Freedom, says Paul, builds unity and brings people together, because it is based on the truth of the gospel (14) and not on the opinion of those with the loudest voices. And the freedom of the gospel means that we needn't be afraid of those who disagree with us and who want to force us to see things their way. At the root of Peter's problem was fear. Maybe he was afraid that his standing in Jerusalem would be diminished if word got back that he ate freely with Gentiles. Maybe he was afraid that he was being led astray by the free and easy atmosphere in Antioch.

But that freedom was based on the gospel that Paul preached – and that Peter himself had agreed on at the Jerusalem meeting. And it's the gospel that gives us our identity as God's people, not our ethnic or religious background, as Paul spells out in the next section of the letter.

Questions

1. What are the issues on which we cannot compromise in our churches today? Are they the same as Paul's?
2. Have we ever publicly opposed a brother or sister over their behaviour in church? Would it ever be right to do so? Under what circumstances?

3. Should we ever restrict our freedom in Christ out of concern for the welfare of our brothers or sisters? (See 1 Corinthians 9:19–20: could Peter not argue that he was simply doing what Paul suggests in this passage?)
4. What are the factors that build unity in the church we attend?

2:15–16

The heart of the matter

Having told his story, Paul now spells out the core of his gospel – and the major plank of his attack on the rival missionaries in Galatia.

It's possible that these verses are a continuation of Paul's report of what he said to Peter when he opposed him to his face in Antioch. But it's equally clear that having lamented his readers' flirtation with heresy and spelled out the origin of his message and his relationship with the Jerusalem church, Paul is now ready to defend his gospel against his opponents. He does so by outlining his case in 2:15–21 and then spelling it out in great detail in 3:1 – 5:12. We tackle his outline in this section (2:15–16) and the next (2:17–21).

He starts with what he is sure his readers and his opponents will 'know' (16). By this he means this is a shared assumption of all Christians – Jewish and Gentile, conservative and radical: our justification is based on faith in Jesus, not obedience to the law (see 'Stop and think', Justification by faith, p. 55).

Who shares this assumption? 'We ourselves' (15) – meaning Paul, Peter and the rival missionaries who are troubling the Galatian churches (see 'Digging deeper', p. 41 for a description of who Paul's opponents were and what they were saying). It clearly doesn't refer to Paul's readers who were for the main part Gentiles, converts from paganism. Why does Paul start here? Probably because, like all good debaters, he begins with the common ground he shares with his opponents. It also tells us – and this point is absolutely crucial – that the dispute between Paul and his opponents was not about how you start the Christian life; rather, it was about how you continue to live the Christian life once you've started (see 'Stop and think' p. 107).

Paul labours the point. Three times he asserts that everyone agrees on how people are justified. It is not by doing the works of the law but by faith in Jesus. Paul uses three terms in particular: 'justified', 'works of the law', 'faith in Jesus'. But before we look at those, we need to look at verse 15 again.

Why does Paul contrast 'we Jews by birth' with 'Gentile sinners'? Hasn't everyone sinned? Doesn't everyone need rescuing by God? Isn't that the reason Jesus came?

The word Paul uses is *hamartōloi*, meaning those who fall short of the mark. It was the term that Jews of the time used to describe the Gentiles, because they were outside the covenant that God had made with Abraham and his descendants and who, therefore, did not live according to the law of Moses or do the works of the law that marked the people of Israel as separate from the rest of the world. It wasn't that they felt the Gentiles sinned and the Jews didn't, but that the law gave the Jews a means of atoning for their sins that was not available to Gentiles.

There is a degree of sarcasm in the way Paul uses the term here. It is a hint that though he is beginning at the place where he and his opponents agree, pretty soon their paths will diverge. He is in effect saying to his readers, 'Did you know that these new teachers see you as sinners and themselves as righteous?' In other words, these rival missionaries view the Galatians as rather second-class, inferior Christians because they are still 'Gentile sinners' in their eyes until they are circumcised and start doing the works of the law (see 'Stop and think', p. 81).

Everyone agrees (16) that we are justified, that is, made right before God, by faith. Whose faith? The answer to that lies in the structure of verse 16. It is what's known as a chiasm, which is easier to see in a diagram than explain in words:

> A: we know a person is justified not by works of the law
>   B: but through the faith of Jesus (*pisteōs Iēsu Christou*)
>   C: And we have come to believe in Christ Jesus
> B^1: so that we might be justified by the faith of Christ
>   (*pisteōs Christou*)
> A^1: and not by doing the works of the law, because no one will be justified by the works of the law.

At the heart of the verse (C – the centre point of the chiasm) is how we come to be justified before God: it is through our faith in Jesus. The phrases either side of the centre point (B, B^1) show us how God can accept us on the basis of our faith: it is through Jesus' faithfulness. The beginning and end of the verse (A, A^1) emphasize that justification happens apart from the works of the law.

The faith in Christ (B^1) may refer to *our* faith in Christ, but I believe – with a good number of writers on Paul – that it makes better sense to hear Paul refer to Jesus' own faith.

What's going on here? Remember Paul is only beginning his rebuttal of the rival missionaries' teaching, a task that will take him until 5:12. But in essence his argument is as follows.

Jesus is the faithful Son of God who gave himself to rescue us from the present evil age (1:4). Here Paul says that our justification – our being declared righteous and hence members of God's people – rests solely, absolutely and only on Jesus' faithfulness to the mission God gave him, that is, giving himself on the cross. The structure of the verse helps us to see this: twice Paul stresses that our justification comes through the faith of Jesus (B and B^1 in the diagram above). The phrase *pisteōs Christou* is often translated 'faith in Christ' but could also be translated 'the faith of Christ', where faith is understood to be Christ's faithfulness to God (see 'Stop and Think', p. 122). Either way our justification is by belief in Jesus, who in faithfulness to God's plan has rescued us through his death on the cross.

As we shall see in the next section and in Part 3, Paul is arguing that Christ is the only faithful member of God's covenant people, the only one who has lived faithfully before God; that everyone else – Jew as well as Gentile – is 'a sinner', that is, they are outside God's covenant people. But at the heart of verse 16 (C in the diagram) is the fact that by our faith in or trust of Jesus, we are counted in the covenant. If we are 'in Christ' by faith, we are part of the covenant people of God, a status that doesn't have anything to do with our ethnicity or our keeping the law.

Indeed, Paul is keen to stress that our faith is not another kind of 'work of the law'. We are not saved by our faith, he says. We are counted righteous by Jesus' faith and our simple trust of him and what he has done. Paul spells this out in 2:17–21 with his graphic description of those in Christ having been crucified with him.

His opponents argued that having put their trust in Jesus, the Galatians needed to do the works of the law – understood to mean getting circumcised, keeping the dietary laws and observing the Sabbath and other special days of the Jewish calendar, and undertaking a Jewish lifestyle of obedience to the commandments. It's as if faith is the door through which you enter the Christian way of life, but in order to live it, you need to do the works of the law. Paul says that to live this way is to devalue the faithfulness of Christ. Indeed, in the next section he argues that it renders the cross meaningless.

Questions

1. What do you think Paul means by 'the faith/faithfulness of Jesus Christ'?

2. How do you feel about the fact that you can do nothing to earn your salvation?
3. What are the 'modern works of the law' we impose on people coming to faith in our churches?
4. What are the things we need to agree on to be able to have fellowship with one another? Is it a long or a short list?
5. If you are studying this as a group, reflect together on how you might present the message of 2:11–16 to your church or a wider group, using drama and a modern setting.

Justification by faith

The great theologians of the Reformation drew on Galatians to form their thinking about justification by faith, understood to mean how I am made right with God when I put my faith in Jesus. But while the language of justification and righteousness is very important in Galatians, its use may be more complex and compelling than the traditional view suggests.

The Greek words that speak about justification and righteousness appear thirteen times in the letter. They are all derived from the same root in Greek: *dikaio-* meaning 'right', 'righteous', 'making right', 'treat as righteous'. The words appear between 2:15 and 5:4, where Paul is spelling out his view of how we become and remain members of God's people. Traditionally this has been spoken of as 'justification' (becoming a Christian, a member of God's people) and 'sanctification' (being made holy through the work of God's Spirit in our lives). Using the English word 'rectify' might give a better sense of Paul's meaning. God rectifies us when we put our trust in Jesus. He continues to rectify us – put right the way we live – as we walk in obedience to his Spirit through our lives.

Paul's use of this language is deeply rooted in his understanding of the covenant between God and his people (Israel). To be marked out as righteous by God meant to be included in the covenant that God had established with Abraham and his descendants. God acted according to his righteousness, which any first-century Jew would have understood to mean God's faithfulness to his covenant. God's people were righteous because they lived within the bounds of the covenant established by the grace of God's calling of Israel. Their response to being included in this covenant was to keep the law God gave the people on Mount Sinai, building on the relationship established with Abraham and marked by circumcision.

The key section is Galatians 2:15–21 where the words appear five times – always rendered 'justify/justified'. It is interesting to note, however, that *dikaiosune*, translated 'justification' in 2:21 (NRSV) is exactly the same word translated 'righteousness' in 3:21. This indicates that in Paul's thinking – as in the thinking of his opponents – there is really no distinction between 'justification' and 'righteousness'. Indeed, it is probably fair to say that Paul doesn't really have a doctrine of justification. Rather he has a doctrine of righteousness of which what we call justification is a part.

Let's look at how Paul uses the language in the four sections where it occurs:

▶ **2:15–21 (5 times):** he stresses that we are 'justified'/'declared righteous' by faith not by the works of the law (see 'Stop and think', p. 81). The faith he is talking about is our trust in what Jesus has achieved through his faithful obedience to God in suffering death on a cross (21). Righteousness comes not through following a legal code but by sharing in the death of Jesus (19–20).

▶ **3:6–11 (4 times):** Abraham is our model for being declared righteous (justified) through faith (6). Gentiles will be justified in the same way (8) – i.e. by faith not by obeying the works of the law. Indeed, those who submit to the law are under a curse because not only will they not be able to keep every detail of it, but God has decreed prior to the law being given that people will be declared righteous only by faith as Abraham was (11).

▶ **3:21-24 (twice):** At the end of Paul's lengthy Bible study, he reiterates that righteousness can't come via the law because the law isn't up to it. Rather, the law was meant to keep us in check until God's way of putting everyone right with him (justifying) was revealed. That way, faith came in Jesus (see 'Stop and think', p. 122 for a discussion about whose faith).

▶ **5:4-5 (twice):** Just as Paul is launching into his discussion of life in the Spirit, he warns his wayward readers that wanting to be made righteous via the law is folly because it cuts us off from Christ – the very one who is able to justify through faith (4). Rather, through the Spirit at work in us we hope for righteousness (5). Paul's point is that through the Spirit we will live so that on the day of judgment God will confirm in reality his verdict that we have received now through faith.

2:17–21

Dying with Christ

Paul drives his point home with an argument that offers his life in Christ as the template for the normal Christian experience.

Paul is still writing in the white heat of his blazing passion about the Galatians' loss of their faith in his gospel (1:6–9). His anger does not help his clarity! But there is a fierce logic to his argument here that drives him to the heart of his understanding of how we live as Christians in the world. Remember, the issue between him and his opponents is not so much how you start the Christian life, but how you live it.

As often happens, Paul becomes aware of a possible objection to his case while he's in the middle of making it (17). So he uses it to push his argument forward (much as he does in Romans 6). Here it's the idea that if we don't need the law to be righteous, that makes us 'sinners' and risks making Jesus a servant of sin.

It's an objection that arises logically enough from the end of verse 16, which literally says 'by works of the law will not be justified all (or any) flesh'. 'All/any flesh' must include 'we ourselves' (15), that is, Jews. So, if no one can both begin and continue the Christian life through the works of the law, then everyone, Jew and Gentile alike, falls into the category of 'sinners', those who are outside God's covenant people. Paul will spell out how this works in chapter 3. Here he is concerned to clear the ground for the key point he wants to make, which is simply this: to suggest Paul's argument makes Christ a servant of sin is complete nonsense ('certainly not' at the end of verse 17 is a very strong negative).

Indeed, to add works of the law to faith in Christ demonstrates the opposite of what the rival missionaries think it does. It shows that we are transgressors rather than righteous (18). We are transgressing in the sense that we are rejecting the way God has chosen to put and keep people in a right relationship with him – namely the faithful death of Jesus (as Paul says in 21 repeating 16). If 'all flesh' cannot be justified by works of the law because God has determined that 'all flesh' will be made righteous on account of Jesus' faithfulness, then to try to begin and continue being righteous through doing works of the law is to build up what God and our trust of him have torn down.

The final nail in the opponents' argument is that the law, according to contemporary Jewish thinkers, while offering life to those within the covenant, offered only death to those outside it. So, if Paul finds himself outside the covenant – with the 'all flesh' of verse 16 – because only Christ, the single faithful descendent of Abraham (as Paul explains in chapter 3), is within the covenant, then the law kills him, for it pronounces death on 'sinners', those outside the covenant community (19a).

But that's okay, says Paul, because in dying to the law, I have come alive to God (19b). How? By being crucified with Christ (19c). It seems as if Paul pulls this phrase out of thin air like a rabbit from a hat to counter the twin problems that he's facing. On the one hand there is the bondage of the rival missionaries' gospel of rules and regulations that would rob these young Christians of the freedom they should enjoy in Christ. On the other hand there lies the danger that, free from works of the law, his young converts will make up their Christian lives as they go along, free from restraint. The technical term for this is 'antinomianism' – the belief that we can behave however we like, regardless of any law.

Paul has been leading up to using this phrase, 'crucified with Christ', since the beginning of the letter. It summarizes his gospel, because it appears at the beginning and end of his defence of it (namely here and in 6:14). It clearly says something fundamental about how he understands his life as a Christian. So how exactly does this phrase rescue him from his dilemma? By describing what has actually happened to him as a result of his faith in Jesus, as he explains in verse 20.

Our faith, says Paul – using himself as the model believer – links us to Jesus' faithful life. Literally Paul says: 'that which now I live in the flesh, by faith I live, that [referring to faith] of the Son of God, the one who loved me and gave himself over on behalf of me.' Again, Paul is stressing – as he did in verse 16 – that it is Jesus' faith that matters here. He lived in utter faithfulness to the calling of God, a calling that led him to the cross to be given over to death to rescue us from the present evil age (see 1:3–4).

So Paul is able to live to God, not because he does the works of the law, but because Christ was faithful in doing God's will, which included suffering death on the cross on our behalf. So Paul now lives, not by what he does – be that works of the law or even his faith – but by what the faithfulness of Jesus achieved. And this is not just how Paul started his Christian life. This is how he lives it every day of his life.

He stresses this point by saying it twice. 'It is no longer I who live, but Christ who lives in me' (20a), and then, repeating the word *sarx* (flesh) from the end of verse 16, he says, 'the life I now live in the flesh I live by the faith of the Son of God' (20b, NRSV). This has huge implications for our lifestyle, as Paul spells out in 5:13 – 6:10.

But the broad outline of those implications is clear from these verses. We live not for ourselves and our agenda – as Paul's opponents did – but 'to God' (NRSV) and his agenda (19b). And if we no longer live – because by faith we have been joined to Christ's death – but Christ lives through us, then our lives will be marked by the same qualities that marked his – and especially by his self-giving love.

This, says Paul, is all of grace (21a), the grace that his readers risk abandoning if they follow the teaching of his opponents (1:6). The grace in question is obviously that of the self-giving love of Jesus (20b). But Paul puts it the way he does in this brief summary of his argument in 2:15–21, in order to show that it is not him but his opponents who 'nullify the grace of God' (21a, NRSV). They argue that God's grace is seen in the provision of the works of the law which the Galatians must do if they want to be sure of their justification. Rot, says Paul; if that were true then Christ died for nothing (21c). Rather, the grace of God is seen and experienced solely in the self-giving love of Jesus. We are justified by that alone and not by anything we do. Adding works of the law nullifies that grace.

Paul will unpack the compressed argument of 2:16–21 in 3:1 – 5:12. But he has laid out the key components of his gospel: namely, we are justified by trusting in the faith of Jesus, that is, his faithfulness to the will of God who sent him; and that we live now not by works of the law but through the faithful life of Jesus being lived through us in our daily lives as we walk with him by faith.

Questions

1. What does it mean to you to have been crucified with Christ?
2. If we have died to the law, what should our attitude to the Old Testament be?
3. What kind of lifestyle should we live if verse 20 is true of us?
4. Are there things we do individually and in our churches that risk nullifying the grace of God (21)?
5. Turn verses 19–20 into a prayer or a song!

FREEDOM AND THE SCRIPTURES

Galatians 3 – 4

3:1–9

God keeping his promise

Having outlined his argument, Paul now earths it in Scripture, taking his readers on a breathtaking ride through the Old Testament.

When he first taught them, Paul would probably have told his Gentile converts the story of Israel from Abraham onwards, in order to give them the broad picture of God's dealings with and plans for his world. It was the back story to the story of Jesus. It was the history within which the life, teaching, death and resurrection of Christ made sense.

But he would have started with Jesus. So, as he reminded the Corinthians, 'I resolved to know nothing while I was with you except Jesus Christ and him crucified' (1 Corinthians 2:2). At the beginning of Galatians 3, he recalls his readers to the moment they first heard the gospel, before his rivals pitched up and confused them with all their talk of the law. And, as ever, he is graphic in his language: 'Before your very eyes Jesus Christ was clearly portrayed as crucified' (1).

It was this preaching that unleashed the power of God in their midst – the coming of the Holy Spirit (2), the working of miracles (5). The gospel preached is God's power for salvation to all who believe, as Paul says in Romans 1:16.

Furthermore, in recalling his readers to the moment they first heard the good news about Jesus, he reminds them of the apocalyptic character of the gospel (see 1:4, 6:15 and 'Stop and think', p. 38). The Holy Spirit was the sign par excellence that the new age longed for by Israel's prophets had at last dawned. And Paul says the Galatians entered this new age, not by doing the works of the law (twice, in verses 2 and 5 – slightly obscured by the NIV as the Greek says 'works of the law' both times), but through believing the Good News about Jesus, the crucified one (2, 5).

How then can these people think that having entered the new age of God's kingdom by faith in Jesus, they would live in it by the law which belongs to the old evil age of sin and death? Paul's only explanation is that someone must have bewitched them. Oh yes, he perfectly believes that the Galatians are acting foolishly (1, 3) and are responsible for following the nonsense spouted by his rivals. And yet he sees something demonic about it as well. How could sensible people trade the freedom of life in the Spirit for the bondage of life under a mountain of rules and regulations that can only bring a curse on them?

Why does Paul use such extreme language? Because he is paving the way for his glorious Bible study which begins in verse 6. The study will be based on Genesis 15 and Deuteronomy 27 – 30 with a bit of Habakkuk and Leviticus thrown in for good measure. And the word he uses for 'bewitched' (unique in the New Testament) appears in the Greek Old Testament only in Deuteronomy 28:53–57.

Paul's Bible study is both immensely subtle in the way it handles Scripture and savage in its assault on the rival teachers. And both the subtlety and the savagery start right at the beginning of chapter 3 and continue through to the end of chapter 4.

In using the word 'bewitched', he is suggesting that powerful forces are at work, confusing his Galatian converts and pointing them to the fact that if they do as his rivals ask them, they will be putting themselves under the curse that falls on all who fail to keep the law at every point.

The context in which the word 'bewitched' appears in Deuteronomy is in the description of the awful things that will befall Israel if they fail to live as God commands. Moses predicts that Israel's rebellion will lead to the land being overrun by its enemies, its cities besieged. In the midst of the siege, the people will resort to cannibalism. And twice (28:54, 56), the text speaks of people casting the evil eye (the same word used in Galatians 3:1) over neighbours and family members in order to survive.

This section of Deuteronomy is the focus of Paul's attention in Galatians 3:10–14. But at the outset he gives his readers a flavour of his argument. In effect, he is saying that the rival missionaries have put the young believers under a curse. It's strong stuff.

But his readers should know better – hence Paul twice calling them foolish (1, 3) – because Paul has already told them about Abraham. His 'consider Abraham' (6) strongly implies that the story of God's call to Abraham – a Gentile like them – was part of the back story Paul had told them as he discipled the young believers in their new faith; he is referring to someone they know about.

Here he draws a stark contrast between Abraham and all that came after him – including Moses and the law. Quoting Genesis 15:6 (6) and 12:3 (8), Paul recalls God's call to and covenant with the Patriarch. As in Romans 4, so here Paul says that Abraham is the model believer for all who come after him – especially Gentiles (7–8). Three times Paul uses the word 'faith' (8, 9) and twice he refers to 'believing' (6,7). The point is simple: being credited as righteous, being part of the people of God, has nothing to do with works of the law and everything to do with faith.

Paul could have left it there and moved on to dealing with life in the Spirit. But he has to account for why God gave the law and how Jesus dealt with sin apart from the law. It's that he turns to in the next section.

Questions

1. What can 'bewitch' people today and deceive them into losing the heart of the gospel?
2. Do we expect God's power to be unleashed when we preach the gospel? How?

3. Paul wants his *Gentile* converts to think of themselves as Abraham's children (see verse 7 and later verse 29). What does it mean to you to think of having Abraham as your 'father'?

4. Think of an area of disagreement in your church: how would Paul's approach here help or hinder in resolving it?

Paul's use of the Old Testament

Much of Paul's argument with his rivals in Galatia centred on the interpretation of the Hebrew Bible. In chapters 3 and 4 in particular, he mounts a sophisticated defence of his gospel, based on a close reading of a number of Old Testament texts.

But his use of the Old Testament is not just about piling up proof-texts to build an argument. Rather, he seeks to show that his gospel is consistent with the narrative sweep of the Hebrew Bible, from the calling of Abraham, through the exodus to exile and return.

Paul is often accused of playing fast and loose with the text of the Old Testament. People say that he twists the meaning of words, that he takes verses out of context, even that he sometimes seems to claim that a passage says the opposite of what it clearly says. But this is grossly unfair.

It's clear that his rivals used Old Testament stories to build their case. So part of Paul's task is to refute their interpretation of these stories and replace it in his readers' minds with his.

There are eleven direct quotes from the Old Testament in Galatians (see table 2) and countless other places where Paul clearly has in mind an Old Testament story or theme – for example 3:14 where Isaiah 44:3 is clearly in Paul's mind, as it contains reference to the Spirit, the blessing and the seed, all of which feature in Paul's argument in this section.

Table 2: Paul's Old Testament quotations

Galatians 2:16	Psalm 143:2
Galatians 3:6	Genesis 15:6
Galatians 3:8	Genesis 12:3; 18:18
Galatians 3:10	Deuteronomy 27:26
Galatians 3:11	Habakkuk 2:4
Galatians 3:12	Leviticus 18:5
Galatians 3:13	Deuteronomy 21:23
Galatians 3:16	Genesis 13:15 (cf. 12:7; 17:7; 22:18)
Galatians 4:27	Isaiah 54:1
Galatians 4:30	Genesis 21:10
Galatians 5:14	Leviticus 19:18

But even this does not account for the influence of Old Testament stories on Paul's argument. For instance, it's clear that Galatians 3 is a sustained reflection on Genesis 15 and especially verse 6. Reference to that story appears explicitly in verses 6–9, 15–20 and 29, but the call of Abraham and the promise of blessing made to him clearly give shape to the whole chapter.

And this gives us three major keys to help us read Paul's quotes from and allusions to the Old Testament.

Key one: the Old Testament is primarily the narrative of God's dealings with people – especially the story of how through Abraham and his descendents God planned to undo the damage to creation caused by people's rebellion and sin. This is why the story of Abraham is so vital in Galatians: it is the paradigm of how God deals with individuals and uses them in his redemption of the created order.

Key two: whenever Paul quotes directly from a story, he intends us to read or know the context of that individual story and how it fits in the narrative sweep of the Hebrew Bible. He is not into proof-texting. Rather, he puts in a direct quote to show us which part of the Old Testament story he is thinking about and how it advances the argument he is making.

Quoting and alluding

So in 3:10 where he quotes Deuteronomy 27:26, Paul expects us to read it in its context. It is the last in the list of curses that will befall the people if they fail to live by the law God has given them when they enter the land. The context tells us that this is not about individual Israelite sin and thus individual Jews being under the curse of law-breaking. Rather it is about the nation. If they fail to live faithfully by the law God has given, they will be carried into exile.

Moreover, Paul expects us to read this text in the light of our knowledge of how the story unfolds. We know the nation did indeed fail to live by the law God gave – despite countless prophets coming with dire warnings about the consequences of their continuing down this road. We know the nation was destroyed and sent into exile – a state that pertained to Paul's day as none of the prophecies about the restoration had yet been fulfilled. Paul expects us to bring all that to the reading of a single well-chosen verse from Deuteronomy.

But direct quotation is not the extent of his use of the Old Testament. Frequently, he intends us to hear echoes of the Hebrew Bible in what he is saying. A good example of this is 3:14, where Paul talks about the cross of Christ opening up the blessing promised to and through Abraham to the Gentiles. The verse ends with the words 'so that by faith we might receive the promise of the Spirit'.

While faith is certainly part of Genesis 15 where we read of God's promise to Abraham, there is no mention of the Spirit. But Paul has in mind the prophecies concerning the restoration from exile such as Isaiah 32:15–17 and Ezekiel 37:1–14, but especially Isaiah 44:3 (in the context of verses

1–5). Here the prophet sees a future where the receiving of blessing is closely tied with God pouring out his Spirit. The other clue to the fact that this is in Paul's mind is that the word for descendents here in the Greek Old Testament is *sperma* ('seed'), the word used in Genesis 12 and 15 – the word that triggers and forms the heart of the next part of his Bible study in 3:15–22.

Key three: Paul sees the Old Testament fulfilled in Jesus and reads it in the light of his ministry – his life, death, resurrection and enthronement as the world's true king. The Old Testament was always leading its readers somewhere. It is incomplete in itself. Paul says that it reaches its climax in Jesus.

And how would Paul expect his Gentile Galatian readers to know all this? Because he told them. Part of his discipling of new converts must have involved filling in the back story of Jesus, showing how he was the fulfilment, the denouement of the story that started with the call of Abraham, the father of all who believe. By believing in Jesus, this story becomes their story.

3:10–14

Christus breaks the curse

God's promise to Abraham was threatened by Israel's continuing exile which kept the Gentiles from enjoying the promise.

For his first readers the transition between verses 9 and 10 must have been very shocking. They were being told by Paul's rivals that, in order to follow God faithfully as disciples of Jesus, they   needed to become part of God's law-defined people, the ethnic descendants of Abraham. The first phrase of verse 10 (literally: 'all who are of the works of the law') means those whose identity is derived from doing the works of the law. But that, says Paul, means going back from the new age of the kingdom of God into the old evil age from which Christ had rescued them (1:4).

In this short section, which continues his reflection on Genesis 15, Paul builds his argument using four Old Testament texts: Deuteronomy 27:26 (10), Habakkuk 2:4 (11), Leviticus 18:5 (12) and Deuteronomy 21:23 (13). His use of these texts is subtle and controversial but their combined weight packs an enormous punch.

All four texts have to do with choosing whether to be faithful to God – often in tough circumstances. So, in Deuteronomy 27 – 30, Moses lays before the people the stark choice: keep the covenant defined by the law in all its detail and be blessed; disregard it and curse will follow as sure as night follows day. The curse includes defeat at the hands of their enemies and exile from the land that God will give them.

Many Jews of Paul's day felt they were still in exile as a result of the nation's disobedience. True, they had returned to the land in the fifth century BC, but they remained under foreign domination (most recently Rome) and the prophecies about the blessings that would follow their restoration to the land – most notably contained in Deuteronomy 30 where Moses looks forward to a renewed covenant when God's law would be written on the hearts of the people (1–14) – had not yet come true. So they felt themselves still under the curse suffered by law-breakers. This was a key motivating factor behind the Pharisees' zeal to keep the law in every detail and exclude from the true people of Israel those who did not follow their example. And it was probably a motive of Paul's rivals.

Paul warns his readers that by embracing the law they would become part of a people (ethnic Israel) whose national way of life was cursed due to their disobedience. The curse had not come on Israel because of the accumulation of lots of individual sins committed by individual Jews. After all, the law made ample provision for sacrifice and forgiveness. Rather, the curse was on the nation of Israel itself for its failure to be the channel of blessing to all the nations of the world, which had been God's intention in calling and making his covenant with Abraham.

And this failure had to do with where people got their primary identity from. Verse 10 opens with the suggestion that Paul's rivals were telling the Galatians that they need to find their identity as God's people through doing the works of the law. By contrast, Paul says that our identity must be derived from our faith in God as Abraham's was (11). He reinforces this by quoting Habakkuk 2:4. The context here is of Israel sliding into judgment at the hands of the Babylonians because of their failure to be faithful to God. When Habakkuk objects that the Babylonians are more sinful than Israel, God replies that the righteous will live by faith – probably understood as both their faith in God and God's faithfulness to them.

By contrast, the people who derive their identity from doing the law must keep it fully or they will not live (Leviticus 18:5 quoted in verse 12). The point is that 'life' – the common theme between Habakkuk and Leviticus – comes not through what we do but who we trust. Paul's rivals probably argued that life came through the law, a view which a surface reading of Deuteronomy would support. But Paul asserts that life comes only through faith, something Moses would have agreed with, for keeping the law was, for Moses, not an end itself, but the sign that Israel trusted in and would be faithful to its redeemer God. The law was the badge of the redeemed not the entry ticket to redemption.

However, Moses himself expected Israel to fail to be faithful and so to bring down on itself all the curses that come from law-breaking (Deuteronomy 30:1–2). More than that, Moses foresaw the new covenant that would be different from the one made with Israel at Sinai because it would be written on the hearts of the people (Deuteronomy 30:1–14). But this new covenant could only come when the exile was finally over. And Paul says that the exile ended on the cross (13).

'Christ' (13) is the Greek for 'Messiah' which means anointed one. Paul understood Jesus to be the king of Israel, the promised Messiah who would rescue the people from exile and bring the blessings of the new age. How did he accomplish this? Through his death on the cross.

In the Old Testament the king was the representative of the people; what happened to him determined the nation's fate. So frequently the prophets spoke of judgment coming on Israel because of the appalling behaviour of its kings (Ezekiel 34). But the Old Testament also pictured how the nation would be blessed when the king lived faithfully before God (for example, Psalm 72). Paul applies this strand of Old Testament thinking to Jesus – with a scandalous twist.

Christ lifts the curse by bearing the curse in his own body on the cross. On a Roman gibbet, symbol of Israel's continuing exile under pagan rule, Israel's king bore the punishment for law-breaking by the nation in order to redeem the nation from slavery. Paul's final quote in this section hints that Jesus became God's rebellious son – Israel was often pictured as God's son and so was its king. The quote from Deuteronomy 21:23 comes at the end of a section dealing with rebellious sons and warning the people not to pollute the land by leaving the dead hanging on trees overnight. In this it echoes 2 Corinthians 5:21.

The cross spells the end of exile, which means that the promise to Abraham that the whole world will be blessed through him can now come true (14a). Paul links the promise with the coming of the Holy Spirit (14b), because he has at the back of his mind a string of Old Testament texts that link the end of exile with the outpouring of God's Spirit on the nations (Isaiah 32:15–17; 44:1–5; Ezekiel 37:1–14). The text at the front of Paul's mind is Isaiah 44:3, which explicitly links the Spirit, the blessing and the seed (descendants), a thought which carries his readers into the next section.

Questions

1. Do you think Paul is fair in the way he uses the Old Testament?
2. Where do we find our primary identity as human beings? Is it through what we do or who we trust? What difference do these two options make to the way we live?
3. How do our actions as God's people (the church) prevent others from sharing the promise to Abraham?
4. What picture of Jesus emerges from these verses? How has he 'redeemed us from the curse of the law'?

3:15–18

The promise and the seed

The promise to Abraham predates the giving of the law and points to a future beyond the law.

Paul knows that his readers – especially the rival teachers – would be bursting with questions and objections at this point. So he softens his tone, calls them  'brothers', and says that he is speaking to them 'in a human way'. This warns us that the analogy Paul is about to use should not be pressed too far lest we make him say things he is not saying.

He likens the covenant God made with Abraham to a human last will and testament. Indeed, the word he uses for 'covenant' – *diatheke* – is the ordinary Greek term for the will someone would write concerning their estate. When the Old Testament was translated from Hebrew into

Greek, however, it was also the term used to translate the Hebrew word for covenant.

So Paul here daringly suggests that the covenant God made with Abraham is like the will that many of his first readers would have drawn up or been the beneficiaries of. And all of them would know that once a will had been written, it could not be altered. Likewise, the covenant God made with Abraham couldn't be changed by anything that happened subsequently – not even the giving of the law.

The promises contained in this covenant were for Abraham and his seed (16). Now the people of Israel understood this to apply to them because 'seed' is a collective noun referring to all Abraham's descendants. It is a perfectly natural and reasonable way to read the Genesis story. Paul, however, asserts that 'seed' is a singular noun referring to one particular descendant of Abraham who would be the primary beneficiary of this will (to continue the human analogy Paul is using). That single descendant is Christ (16c).

To modern ears, Paul's argument here appears odd, even twisted. But it's actually very clever. Paul knows that seed is a collective noun, legitimately understood to refer to a collection of people. He has already said that Abraham has many children – 'those who believe' (3:7) – and his argument will climax by asserting that Abraham's seed includes everyone who is in Christ (3:29). And Paul's rivals know – because they would have been well versed in the interpretative methods of the rabbis – that what Paul is doing here is perfectly acceptable and in line with contemporary ways of reading and expounding texts. Indeed, he is building on an Old Testament tradition, which asserted that King David was the 'seed' through whom God would fulfil his covenant with Abraham (2 Samuel 7:12–14; Psalm 89:3–4). And Paul has already argued that Christ is Israel's representative because he was its rightful king.

His understanding of the single 'seed' is a vital building block in his argument that the one God is seeking a single worldwide family which relates to him the way Abraham did – namely by faith and not by works of the law. Jesus, the seed, relates to God in this way.

Having established that, he returns to his human analogy. Note again the gentleness of his tone – 'what I mean is this' (17a). It's very different from the combative way his argument began at the start of the chapter. He asserts that the law, coming 430 years after the covenant was made with Abraham (his dating is based on Exodus 12:40–41), cannot set it aside and change its terms. The promise – based on grace and faith – is not altered by the law and the works associated with it.

Because Paul is using the picture of a human will, which has to do with the inheritance of an estate, he uses this language to describe the effect of the promise God made to Abraham (18). But the term 'inheritance' – which becomes important later in his argument (3:29, 4:1–7, 30) – should not be seen as introducing a fresh idea. Rather, it is just another way of describing the outcome of the promise – namely that people are put and kept right with God by their faith.

And again he makes a simple and stark contrast: the inheritance comes not through the law but through the promise. There is a close parallel between 3:18 and 2:21. In 2:21, he argues that if being put right with God came through the law, then Christ died for nothing. Here he argues that if the inheritance came through the law, the promise has been nullified. Neither can be true.

The final clause of verse 18 is interesting. Literally Paul says the inheritance was 'graced' to Abraham. The verb is perfect tense, indicating a past action with continuing effects in the present. In other words, the promise was given by God to Abraham as an act of grace and received by him by faith – and all who come after him receive it in the same way.

Paul is summarizing everything he's argued about Abraham, picking up points in verses 14, 16 and 6–9 and paving the way for his daring – and possibly dangerous suggestion – that the law was a provisional arrangement while the promise was awaiting its fulfilment in the 'seed', who was long-expected and longed-for and who has finally come: namely Jesus.

Questions

1. Can you summarize what Paul is saying here about the relationship between the covenant with Abraham and the law of Moses?
2. How well do you know the story of Abraham? In what ways does he illustrate being a Christian today?
3. What is our 'inheritance' (verse 18)?
4. You have one minute in which to explain how we relate to God through Jesus. What do you say?

3:19–25

Putting the law in its place

Paul's argument that the promise does not need the law in order to be fulfilled begs the question of why the law was given in the first place.

If the promise to Abraham is fulfilled apart from the law, 'what, then, was the purpose of the law?' (19). This question has been hovering in the background for some time now. More than that, the law appears to be a hindrance, unable to confer the Holy Spirit (2–5), bringing a curse on those under it (10), promising life but withholding it (12–13) and apparently thwarting God's promise (15–18). Paul now faces this question head-on, suggesting the law had two purposes. One is spelled out in verses 19–20, the other in 21–25.

The law's provisional nature is indicated at the start of the section – 'until the Seed … had come' (19b), but its purpose according to this verse is hardly clear. Paul says it was 'added because of transgressions'. Presumably by 'added' Paul means that God put the law in place *after* making the promise to Abraham but *before* that promise was honoured, for a specific and time-limited period.

The word 'transgressions' is the clue to Paul's meaning here. One can only transgress if there is a rule to break or a line to cross. So Paul is not saying that sin didn't exist until there was law. Sin is universal, affecting those with and those without the law. Rather he is suggesting two things. First, that the law identifies and even classifies sin. This is similar to his argument in Romans 4:15 and 7:7–13. Secondly, that the law restrains sinful behaviour by pointing out what is sinful so that we might avoid it. He spells this out in verses 23–25.

He seems to put a distance between God and the giving of the law by his curious phrase at the end of verse 19. The mediator was Moses, and Deuteronomy 33:2 mentions the involvement of angels. Is Paul suggesting that God was less involved in the giving of the law than he was in the making of the promise to Abraham? The phrase 'it was added' would suggest not. This is the way a pious Jew of Paul's day would refer to the action of God – it was known as the 'divine passive'. But his reference to angels and a mediator does pave the way for his next damning criticism of the law – namely its failure to create one people for the one God.

This seems to be the gist of the somewhat baffling sentence that follows (20). The final phrase of the verse echoes the Shema (Deut 6:4). But what of the rest? The oneness of God is linked to the singleness of the seed (16) and the oneness of God's family in Christ (29). Paul seems to be suggesting that the law, associated as it was with ethnic Israel, indeed dividing that people off from all the other peoples of the world, could not, by its very nature, create the single people on earth that God desired. Indeed, as the Galatians were finding out all too painfully, the law brought division, cutting one group off from another – the very opposite of God's intention in his promise to Abraham.

So, is the law a problem because it appears to thwart the promise (21a)? This would only be true if the law had been given to 'impart life' (21b). But this was never the intention. Rather, the law was to show that life had been imparted to Israel by God's rescue of them from slavery in Egypt until such time as his promise to Abraham was fulfilled.

It's important to see the apocalyptic language of the two ages (see 'Digging deeper', p. 38) lurking in the background here. Paul uses it in a rather novel way, however. He takes the idea of the present evil age (1:4) and suggests that the law – here the word 'Scripture' (22) is being used as a synonym for law – has a role in making it plain for all to see that this is the age in which we live. It is similar to his argument in Romans 7:7–10 where the law acts to label behaviour so we know that it's against what God wants.

The law confines us, says Paul. It keeps the old order – including Israel – in a state of sin until such time as God could deal with it. That time (anticipating 4:4) is the coming of Jesus. The law – which Israel saw as a protective fence keeping it safe from sin – was in fact the very thing that kept Israel imprisoned in sinfulness (see Romans 3:9). But in keeping all creation in bondage to sin, the law did what God wanted it to until he honoured his promise to Abraham, and in Christ took the curse of the law and set the people of faith free from the enslaving power of sin, death and the law.

Three times in verses 22, 23 and 24 Paul repeats the same thing: namely that the law keeps us prisoner in sin until the promise is honoured through the faith of Abraham's seed. It is important to note that verse 22 – like 2:16 – refers to the faith *of* Jesus, by which Paul means Christ's faithful obedience to his calling in which we put our trust (see 'Stop and think', p. 122).

In verse 23 the stress is on waiting for God to act – again a very apocalyptic thought. 'The faith' referred to here is almost certainly again the faith of Jesus mentioned in the previous verse.

In verse 24 the idea is that the law demonstrates our utter helplessness. The law is our 'disciplinarian' (*paidagōgos* does not mean teacher though we get the English word 'pedagogue' from it; rather, it refers to the household slave responsible for looking after young children and keeping them in check). The NIV is wrong to suggest that the law 'leads us to Christ' because that is not what Paul has been arguing so far – quite the opposite, in fact. Rather, the phrase means 'until Christ came' (as in the NRSV).

At best, says Paul, the law had a negative, restraining role until Abraham's seed appeared. 'Now that faith has come' (25a) – again a reference to Jesus' faithfulness as well as our response of faith (24c) – we don't need a guardian. This is the punchline as far as Paul's first readers and the rival teachers are concerned. To put yourself under the law, under its negative, protective custody, is to step back into the old world order of sin. Why would you do that when you could stay put in God's new world order of grace and promise through faith?

Questions

1. As Christians, do we still need the Old Testament and the law in particular? What would you say to someone who uses the Psalms in prayers but ignores the rest of the Old Testament?
2. What is the relevance of the Ten Commandments for us today? Have they been 'left behind' with the rest of the law?
3. What is the link between Jesus' faith and our faith?

The works of the law

A key plank in Paul's case against his rivals at Galatia was that Christian justification was based on faith and not on 'works of the law'. Paul's rivals argued that, having joined the covenant people through faith in Jesus, all Gentile converts should now start to practise the 'works of the law' (*erga nomou*), because these are required by God.

The phrase appears four times in two crucial passages (2:15–16 and 3:1–5) and is rendered either as 'observing the law' (NIV) or more literally as 'the works of the law' (NRSV).

▶ **2:15–16:** Outlining what Paul and Peter agreed on after the so-called 'incident at Antioch' (2:11–14), the apostle says that 'we know' that justification comes through faith (understood as Jesus' faithfulness and our trust in him – see 'Stop and think', p. 122) not through 'works of the law'. The clue to the meaning of this phrase lies in the previous verse (2:14) where Paul challenges Peter over his withdrawal from table fellowship with Gentiles with the words 'How is it, then, that you force Gentiles to follow Jewish customs?' (The custom in question here is eating with Gentiles.)

It seems that 'the works of the law' were those practices that identified Jewish people and distinguished them from their Gentile neighbours – things such as circumcision, the Old Testament dietary laws, the Sabbath and various festivals linked to the calendar.

Of course, no one thought that these customs were all God wanted. But these 'works' were the essential signs of covenant membership for Jews, required by the law. So the delegation from James (2:12) and the rival missionaries were saying: once you put your trust in Jesus, you will naturally do these things to show that you have become Jews, that is, members of

God's covenant people. But for Paul covenant membership is now defined just by faith, and not at all by being Jewish (albeit *Christian*-Jewish).

▶ **3:1–5:** At the beginning of his Bible study, Paul expresses astonishment that the Galatians are departing from the gospel he preached to them – which obviously said nothing about adopting a Jewish lifestyle – circumcision, dietary rules, Sabbaths or special festivals.

Twice he asks them whether the benefits of being in Christ – namely receiving the Spirit and God working miracles – came as a result of them doing 'the works of the law'. The answer he expects, of course, is no. It's clear to Paul that if God gives his Spirit and works miracles on the basis of people's faith, the works of the law belong to this present age rather than God's future breaking in to the present time through Jesus.

The works of the law then are the things that the law required of God's people under the old covenant – the things that would mark them out as 'Jews'. No, says Paul: these things are not part of what God is doing through Jesus, namely creating a people who relate to God solely through faith as Abraham did.

The one promised family

Having begun his argument by reminding the Galatians of when they first heard the gospel, he concludes it by recalling their baptism.

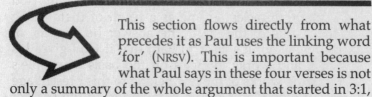

This section flows directly from what precedes it as Paul uses the linking word 'for' (NRSV). This is important because what Paul says in these four verses is not only a summary of the whole argument that started in 3:1, but flows naturally from what he has just said.

We are no longer under the law's supervision (25) because we are children of God. (The word 'sons' is used in 26 because Paul is about to talk about inheritance, something usually reserved for sons; but his argument here clearly includes women as we'll see when we get to verse 28.) And because we are in Christ we are Abraham's seed and heirs, according to the promise God made to Abraham *before* the law was given (29).

Having holed his rivals' arguments below the waterline, he sinks them with this summary of his case: 'in Christ' (he stresses this by saying it three times in four verses) we already have what, according to his rivals, we need the works of the law in order to obtain.

Paul's summary is magnificently simple and theologically rich. 'All' – the word is emphatically at the beginning of the sentence in the Greek – who have faith in Christ are *already* children of God; they don't need to do anything else to fully join Abraham's family.

The phrase 'sons of God' was used in the Old Testament and in the Jewish tradition with which Paul and his rivals grew up to describe Israel as God's elect people. Paul is telling his Gentile readers that they are a part of Israel by virtue of faith – both Jesus' and theirs – a thought he will flesh out in 4:4–7. This picks up Paul's assertion in 3:7 that those who have faith in Jesus are sons of Abraham – again a favoured way for ethnic Israel to describe itself.

To reinforce his point, Paul takes his hearers back to their baptism. The chapter opened with Paul asking the Galatians to recall the time they first heard the gospel of Jesus preached to them (3:1). Now he draws his argument to a close by asking them to remember their baptism, that act through which as believers they consciously and publicly affirmed the lordship of Jesus.

At that moment, he says, they were clothed with Christ (27). This recalls various places in the Old Testament where Israel was pictured as being clothed with something of God (for instance his 'righteousness' and 'salvation' in Psalm 132:9, 16; Isaiah 61:10). But Paul talks of being clothed with a person – namely Christ. This is yet another way in which the apostle speaks of the close union that believers enjoy with their Lord (see 2:20).

Through baptism Christians take on a new identity. From now on they are neither Jew nor pagan; they are Christian. Paul spells this out in verse 28 by speaking of the abolition of all the key social distinctions.

But what precisely does he have in mind? Answer: nothing less than the new creation. In Christ this is already happening, he says. We see it at work in the abolition of the distinctions that cause tension and conflict in our world through Jesus (28).

The distinction between Jew and Gentile was the very one that his rivals wished to reinforce by getting his readers to submit to the works of the law (see 'Stop and think' p. 81). Paul suggests that what they want is a return to the past, whereas in Jesus these distinctions are irrelevant (5:6; 6:15; see Ephesians 2:11–22).

In baptism all get equally wet because all are equally in need of salvation. So the rich, slave-owning class is no better off than poor slaves. And because they all come in the

same way, there should be no distinctions between them
once they've come. Paul does not spell out how this col-
lapse of social class divisions works itself out in the
church, though he does spell out an ethic of mutual service in 5:13 – 6:10, which makes big demands on every-
body, but especially on the rich.

The final distinction is written into the very fabric of
creation. Paul subtly changes the wording in this third
couplet. The first two follow a 'neither ... nor' pattern
(neither Jew nor Greek, slave nor free); the third says literally 'there is not male *and* female', wording that echoes
Genesis 1:27. Clearly Paul means more than simply there
should be equality between the sexes in the church –
something indicated by his practice (see, for example
Romans 16). He is reinforcing his belief that in Christ the
new creation has begun.

The 'works of the law' made a distinction between male
and female because circumcision applied only to males.
But baptism applies to males and females without distinction. The church is a foretaste of this new creation order
and thus it should be a place of harmony and equality. All
(26) are welcome in God's new people regardless of ethnicity, class and gender. The key fact about their identity is
that they are all equally in Christ.

The final sentence of the chapter wraps up its whole
argument. In 3:16 he has asserted that Christ was
Abraham's seed. Here he says that all who 'belong to
Christ' are Abraham's seed. In 3:18 he had told his original hearers that Abraham became an heir through his
faith. Here he says the same is true of all who are in Christ.
And because we are one new person in Christ, there is no
need for any of us to observe the works of the law as
touted by Paul's rivals.

Questions

1. How do you understand baptism?
2. 'You are one in Christ Jesus' (28). Turn this into a

'practical code' for your church: how will you live as one in Christ?

3. What do these verses teach us about the role of women in the church?
4. 'Neither Jew nor Greek' (28). Is Paul denying any special significance or role in the Lord's plans for Jews and the nation of Israel today?

4:1–11

The Spirit of sonship

Paul continues to unpack what it means to be 'in Christ', now focusing on how the Spirit confirms that we are God's children.

At the beginning of chapter 3, Paul asked two questions about the Galatians' Christian experience. The second – whether God worked miracles among them because they did the works of the law (3:5) – he dealt with in the rest of chapter 3. Now he returns to the first: did they receive the Spirit by doing works of the law or by faith (3:2)?

If chapter 3 was about the contrast between faith and law, chapter 4 opens with a contrast between law and Spirit in an argument that paves the way for Paul's exposition of life in the Spirit in 5:13 – 6:10.

It is clear from his opening phrase (4:1) that Paul is continuing the Bible study and its application that he began in 3:6. He is explaining what has happened as a result of the Galatians' faith in the Messiah, and in particular what it means to be a 'son' in contrast to a slave. He will return to this contrast at the end of the chapter (4:21–31).

Here he is continuing to stress that Jew and Gentile become sons in the same way: by the operation of God's Spirit sent into the hearts of those who put their trust in Jesus (6). He describes the different journeys these two groups make to this same destination. In verses 1–5 he speaks to and about Jewish believers. In verses 8–11 he speaks to Gentile converts. In verses 6–7 he expounds the common destination these two groups reach through faith in Jesus.

He is equally keen to undermine his rivals' teaching that sonship comes through doing works of the law. And he does so by consigning the law to this present evil age – we're in the world of apocalyptic thinking here – rather than the new age of the Spirit brought about by Jesus' faithfulness.

Speaking to Jews – and hence mainly to his rivals since most of the Galatian Christians were Gentiles – he reminds his readers that God fulfilled his promise to send a Messiah (4) to redeem the ethnic descendants of Abraham (5) trapped in the spiral of failure and curse associated with the law (see 3:10–14).

But what is most shocking to his rivals is that he suggests the law is part of the present evil age, not part of God's future associated with Jesus. He does this by reminding them that as children awaiting their inheritance (1), they were under the law's guardianship (2; see 3:23–25) and then telling them that they were slaves to 'the basic principles of the world' (3). Notice the emphasis Paul gives to the Jews being slaves and subject people (1, 2, 3).

The word Paul uses in verse 3 is *stoicheia* – the same word he uses in verse 9 to speak of Gentile enslavement. The word means 'basic or primitive elements'. In a sense Paul is only saying what he said in 3:22–25 that the law gave a basic code to walk by until the Messiah came. But he is saying more than this. The *stoicheia* were also understood in spiritual terms. They are another way of speaking about the spiritual 'principalities and powers' that keep the world in bondage to darkness and sin (see Ephesians 6:12).

It was into such a world that God sent his Son. The language of verse 4 is highly apocalyptic: the 'fullness of time' (NRSV) suggests that the coming of Jesus ushered in the turn of the ages. And the idea of the Son being sent from heaven to redeem the world imprisoned by the *stoicheia* is an idea drawn from the apocalyptic vision that God would step in to set the world right. This was a core part of the early Christians' understanding of the coming of Jesus (see Romans 8:15–17; John 3:16–17; 1 John 4:9–10).

The shocking implication of Paul's thinking is simple: how could the Galatians want to have anything to do with the very forces that kept them slaves until Jesus came? And yet if they submit to the rivals' teaching, this is exactly what they'll be doing. And Paul doesn't leave us to draw this inference; he spells it out in 4:8–11.

Addressing his Gentile readers directly, he reminds them that as pagans they too were slaves to spiritual forces. They were in an even worse state than Jewish people because they did not know who the true God was (8a). But through their conversion they became part of God's elect people (9) – that is the idea behind the phrase 'or rather are known by God'. To be known by God is one of the Old Testament's ways of describing the chosen people; they are the one people out of all the peoples of the world that God has chosen to know, to have a relationship with (see for example, Deuteronomy 7:7 and Amos 3:2).

Then he asserts that to follow his rivals' teaching and submit to doing the works of the law would mean being enslaved by the *stoicheia* all over again. The *stoicheia*, which lurked in and behind the paganism from which Jesus rescued them, also lay in wait in the teaching of his rivals.

Indeed, Paul fears that they are already coming under their spell (see 3:1) because they are observing a liturgical calendar (10). They haven't yet submitted to circumcision's knife but they are close. And Paul is close to despair about them (11).

The reason for his despair is spelled out at the heart of

this section. Through faith in Jesus, his hearers have been rescued from the *stoicheia* and brought into close and intimate relation to God through the Spirit (6–7). But they are about to throw it all away.

He has established that we are sons because of our trust in Jesus (3:26–29). Now he spells out how that sonship is made real in our lives through the work of the Spirit (4:6; see Romans 8:15–17).

As God sent Jesus, so he sent into our hearts his Spirit (6a), who speaks to us at the core of our being in such a way that it makes us cry out aloud that we are children of God (6b). More than that, the Spirit confirms that we are no longer slaves, but sons and heirs of the promise God made to Abraham that his family would inherit the earth (3:29; see Romans 4:13).

Why on earth would anyone want to be a slave again? Yet that was what his rivals were offering Paul's young converts. And it's breaking his heart.

Questions

1. Where can we see 'the elemental principles' at work in our world to enslave people?
2. Paul was deeply worried about the Galatian Christians. See also 5:2–4. Must we conclude that it is possible to lose our salvation? What makes it secure (as in Romans 8:31–39)?
3. Paul writes much elsewhere about the experience of the Holy Spirit. But how would you sum up his teaching in this passage? What does God's Spirit do in and through us?

4:12–20

Paul's heart on his sleeve

Having applied the theology, Paul now makes a personal plea to his readers to grasp what has happened to them in Christ.

Paul reveals here that his passion was not just for the truth of the gospel but also for the lives of these people. He gave a hint of what was to come in verse 11; now he pours out his heart in a mixture of contempt for his rivals and tender parental concern for his converts. This is one of two sections – the other being 5:7–12 – where his personal feelings erupt, and we're given a glimpse of the great apostle's passionate heart.

Verse 12 is the first direct appeal Paul makes in the letter. But it's not entirely clear what he's urging his readers to do! Paul often encouraged his churches to copy his behaviour (1 Corinthians 4:16; 11:1; Philippians 3:17; 1 Thessalonians 1:6; 2:14; 2 Thessalonians 3:7, 9) – something we might struggle with but which was commonplace for teachers in the ancient world.

But here he gives the call an eye-popping twist. 'Become like me,' he cries, 'for I became like you.' What does he mean? Probably that when he came to their towns, he lived like a Gentile in order not to put a stumbling block in the way of these people seeing and responding to Jesus. It was 1 Corinthians 9:21 in action. It was costly for him as he's already told them in 2:11–14 – it caused a rift with his friends.

Now, however, those same converts are about to become law-observant under the influence of Paul's rivals. And he begs them not to (12a), because if they do, it will be a personal slight to him as well as a catastrophe for their faith.

This is probably what he means by the phrase 'You have done me no wrong' at the end of the verse.

He then reminds them of their first meeting. He is constantly taking his hearers back to the beginning of their Christian experience. In 3:1 he reminded them of their first hearing of the gospel; in 3:26–29 of their baptism; in 4:6 of their experience of the Spirit. Now he reminds of them of the first time they set eyes on him (13–15).

Where the NIV speaks of 'an illness' (13) and the NRSV 'a physical infirmity', the Greek literally says 'a weakness of the flesh'. Elsewhere when Paul talks about his weakness, it is usually in connection with suffering persecution because of his preaching of the gospel (see, for example, 2 Corinthians 10:29–30; 12:5, 9, 10; 13:4). He uses the same language to speak of Christ's death (1 Corinthians 1:18 – 2:5; 2 Corinthians 13:4).

So it is likely that here he is reminding the Galatians that when he came the first time, he bore in his body the marks of battles he'd had with his opponents. After all, in 6:17 he talks of bearing in his body the marks of Jesus, surely a reference to the effects of persecution.

Verse 14 suggests that this approach is right. Taking the second half first, Paul is saying that when the Galatians saw him and heard his message, they responded along these lines: 'what he's saying must be true, look at what he's prepared to suffer for it'. In a very real sense, Paul's physical appearance powerfully reinforced the content of his message.

This suggests that the first half of the verse probably has to do with the Galatians themselves being prepared to risk the same sort of suffering by responding positively to Paul's preaching. Paul tends to use the words 'a trial' in the sense of test or temptation (see 6:1; 1 Corinthians 10:13). So the meaning here is twofold. The first is as we've just suggested that the Galatians were impressed by what Paul was prepared to suffer for his faith. The second is the Old Testament idea that God's people will suffer because of their witness to his truth and justice (see, for example, Isaiah 53).

So, Paul is saying that when he came and preached, they faced a choice, a test in the apocalyptic language of the letter, and they chose to believe him. Indeed they welcomed him as though he were Christ himself (14c).

More than that, they reached out to him to care for his physical wounds as he shared his life-changing message with them. This appears to be the meaning of verse 15. The reference to eyes is probably not a hint about his physical condition, but a proverbial saying much like the contemporary phrase 'you'd have given your right arm for me'. Paul is saying that a strong bond of friendship was forged between them and it brought them joy (15a).

But now, that friendship has been shattered by the teaching of his rivals, which has robbed them of their joy (15a) and turned them against Paul. It is possible that they don't feel any different towards Paul than they did then, but that's because they don't realize that in embracing his rivals' teaching, they are piercing his heart with a dagger as well as endangering their salvation.

So Paul spells it out (17). His rivals do not have the Galatians' best interests at heart. Being zealous (three times in two verses) is good providing what we're zealous about is worthwhile. Paul has already admitted that he was once zealous about the wrong things (1:13–14) and tried to destroy what he now commits his life to building – namely the church. Now his rivals will destroy what he has built in Galatia if his readers allow them to, through their misguided zeal for the law.

But it is good to be zealous for the things that matter (18) – by which we suppose he means the applying of his gospel and the living of life in the Spirit. He will spell all this out shortly.

He is zealous for them to the best purpose of all – namely that of Christ being formed in them. The tone of his appeal is amazing. First, he calls his readers 'my dear children', the tenderest language he uses in this letter. Then he likens himself to their mother! (see 1 Thessalonians 2:7). He is in labour pains until Christ is formed in them. Again, the language of being in labour is drawn from Jewish and Christian apocalyptic thinking about the turn of the ages. Paul uses the same image in Romans 8:22 to speak of the work of the Spirit in creation.

But Paul's image here is more than just about the birth of individual Christians. The 'you' at the end of verse 19 is plural. So Paul is here talking about the forming of communities of Christians which reflect the character and life of Christ in their relationships with one another – something the presence of his rivals is threatening. Again, Paul is pointing ahead to 5:13 – 6:10, where he tackles all this in detail.

Questions

1. Paul tells the Galatians to 'become as I am' (12). In what ways do you find Paul's example inspiring in this passage?
2. In what ways does Paul set us an example in dealing with dispute, divisions and arguments between Christians – not just in this passage but in the letter as a whole?
3. In verse 19, Paul uses the image of childbirth to describe his relationship with the Galatian Christians. Is all ministry like giving birth? What does this suggest about the Christian life?

4:21–31

Two sons, two destinies

Paul returns to his Bible study with a final *tour de force* of scriptural interpretation that turns the tables on his rivals.

Having looked at the Old Testament in terms of Abraham's faith and God's promise, Israel's failure to keep the law and Christ's death to redeem everyone from the curse of that failure, Paul turns to rebut his rivals' strongest claim. They argued that Abraham circumcised his son, and so everyone who claims to be part of his family should be circumcised.

Paul chooses to do this by expounding an unlikely passage – Genesis 21 (though the whole sweep from 16 – 21 is in mind). He offers an audaciously radical re-interpretation of it through the lens of Isaiah 40 – 55 (he quotes 54:1) and the work of Christ. It's eye-popping stuff, so we need to read it carefully!

Still addressing his readers directly and personally – 'tell me, you …' (21a) – he asks whether they 'hear' what the law says (21b – it's important to remember that most people will have heard rather than read the Scriptures and this letter). He's using 'law' in two senses. The first mention refers to the law as moral code and lifestyle marker, and in Galatians this is always negative. The second refers to the whole Torah, the first five books of our Old Testament. Here he's paving the way for his daring question in verse 30 at the end of his exposition.

The Galatians must have been very familiar with this story. Paul no doubt told it to them, and his rivals certainly used it as the basis for their appeal to them, so Paul is able to provide a brief summary of it (22). Notice that neither of the women are named. Verse 23 sets up a contrast between 'flesh' (the NIV's 'in the ordinary way' is not as good as the NRSV's 'according to the flesh') and 'promise' which looks back to 3:6–9, 28–29.

Having reminded them of the basic outline, Paul tells them he's going to use the story figuratively (24). He doesn't mean that the original story was an allegory. Rather, he's suggesting that in the light of subsequent events, especially the cross, the story can be read symbolically.

The two women – still unnamed – represent two covenants: The first mentioned is the covenant made on Mount Sinai with Moses. Shockingly, Paul states explicitly what he implied in 4:1–11 – namely that the law is associated with slavery not freedom. And finally Paul names the woman associated with it – Hagar. We need to pause to take in the shock his original hearers would have felt as these words were read. They were expecting Sarah to be the one associated with the giving of the law. But no, it's Hagar, the slave woman.

It's important to read what Paul is saying in this verse correctly. He is not talking about an old covenant and a new one. We should not, therefore, read it to say that the old covenant was with the Jews and the new one is with Christians. Rather, Paul, a Jewish Christian, is arguing with other Jewish Christians about how to read the Old Testament story – and in particular the story of the covenants with Abraham and Moses – in the light of the coming of Christ.

And the key here is which way of reading this story leads to slavery and which to freedom. Paul is adamant that his reading sets people free while that of his rivals enslaves. Hence the first blow landed against his rivals at the end of verse 24 with the naming of Hagar.

It's likely that 'bears children' (24) in Paul's figurative reading of this story is a reference to the outcome of missionary preaching. Paul's preaching leads to free-born sons and heirs, that of his rivals to slaves. He picks up the graphic image of 4:19 and warns his readers again of the danger they're in by paying heed to his rivals.

He spells out how his reading works by linking Hagar directly with Mount Sinai and present-day Jerusalem. Mount Sinai is where the law was given (see Exodus 19 – 20). The slave woman corresponds to the law that enslaves and a city that is in effect in captivity to Rome. His argument looks back to his treatment of Deuteronomy 27 – 31 in 3:10–14, where he pointed out that Israel was still effectively 'in exile', which is probably what he means by the phrase 'she is in slavery with her children' (25).

It's almost as if Paul is compiling two lists of opposites: on the one hand stands Hagar, Ishmael (her disinherited son), the flesh, Sinai and present-day Jerusalem; on the other hand (as verse 26 spells out) stands Sarah (still unnamed but strongly implied), Isaac, promise, Spirit and 'the Jerusalem above'. This picture of Jerusalem is derived from the prophets (especially Ezekiel 40 – 48 and Isaiah 40 – 55) and appears elsewhere in the New Testament to describe Christian hope (Hebrews 12:22; 13:14; Revelation 21:1–5).

That this is what Paul has in mind becomes clear as he quotes Isaiah 54:1 (27). In Isaiah 40 – 55, Sarah, the barren woman, was a picture of Jerusalem in exile (see, for instance, 51:1–3). The same long section contains the promise to increase Zion's children by bringing in the Gentiles (49:6; 51:4–5; 52:10; 54:2–3; 55:5). Paul quotes Isaiah 54:1 to evoke this whole theme of God restoring Israel by bringing the Gentiles into it as the fulfilment of his promise to Abraham (see Genesis 12:1–3).

He drives his point home with a direct appeal (28) as he's done before (3:26; 4:6) to his readers to recognize who they are in Christ. Those 'in the line of Isaac' (better than the NIV's 'like Isaac') are heirs of the promise (3:6–9, 28–29).

And with that, Paul has turned the story on its head, for uncircumcised Gentiles are in the line of Isaac, not circumcised Jews, because Isaac's line has to do with faith and promise not with the law and its works.

The rivalry of the brothers (29) is used as a picture of persecution. Those who, like Paul, preach the gospel of freedom are persecuted by those who preach a message of slavery. Paul was once one of these, as he's already reminded them (1:13–14). He persecuted the church precisely because Christians polluted the land of Israel by not upholding the law and its works but allowing Gentiles entry by faith alone. Since his call he's been persecuted by those who resist his insistence that Jesus is the fulfilment of the promise to Abraham and those in him are heirs of that promise in the line of Isaac (4:12–14; 5:11; 6:17).

So he reaches a dramatic conclusion. Having reversed the polarity of the story by making uncircumcised Gentiles the heirs of Isaac and his free mother, he uses the story's own punchline to implore his readers to send his rivals packing (30; Genesis 21:10)!

Finally, he summarizes his whole argument as well as this section in a statement using first person plural verbs (31). It's an inclusive statement of freedom in which Paul says that everyone who follows his gospel will be set free from the curse of sin and death, and enjoy the benefits of the promise God made to Abraham. He spells this out further in the next section.

Questions

1. What do you think is the best way of dealing with people who teach things that aren't in line with Scripture?
2. Is it possible to be a Christian and still be in slavery? If so, what things might enslave us?
3. Is Paul fair in his reading of Genesis 21? What controls are there on such readings of the Bible?
4. What does this passage say about the relationship between Christians and Jews?

FREEDOM AND THE SPIRIT

Galatians 5 – 6

5:1–6

Christt sets us free!

The conclusion of Paul's Bible study is that Christ sets us free. Any other 'gospel' would be a return to slavery.

Having completed his Bible study, Paul now spells out its implications for Christian living. He does this first negatively, imploring his readers to reject the teaching of his rivals (5:1–12), before going on to spell out positively how living by the Spirit means we are able to use our Christian freedom to serve one another (5:13 – 6:10).

Galatians 5:1 is the hinge on which the letter swings, a ringing declaration of the freedom Christ has won for us, which serves as a fitting, one-sentence summary of his complex and lengthy Bible study in chapters 3 and 4. At the same time it is the introduction to his teaching on Christian living which will take up most of the rest of the letter.

Paul has twice spoken of Christ redeeming us (3:13; 4:4–5). This means we are free. More than that, because we are sons and daughters of God (3:29; 4:6–7), we should stand firm and resist anyone's attempts to enslave us. This talk of freedom builds on the key Old Testament theme of exodus and return from exile so prominent in chapter 3. It reminds us to keep in view the twin aspects of freedom: a backward glance that tells us what we have been freed from (in our case, sin and the present evil age); and a forward look at what we are set free for (enjoyment of the life of the world to come now through the cross and Holy Spirit).

Immediately Paul launches into the negative implication of our freedom, namely that we should not be circumcised (2–3). He begins by repeating his name (2; see 1:1), reminding his readers that he is their founding apostle, their parent in the faith (cf. 4:19). And he repeats himself for effect: what he is saying here is so important. Circumcision is not a discrete act but a doorway into an alternative way of being God's people – which Paul has already established is no way at all. People who are circumcised are 'obliged' (3b, NRSV) to keep the entire law. In effect, says Paul, for the Galatians to be circumcised is like going back to Egypt or Babylon, back to slavery.

It's worth noting that although the issue of circumcision has lurked in the background of the letter since 2:3, this is the first time Paul names it as the crunch issue. He has suggested that his readers are slipping into slavery by observing special days (4:10). But here he stresses that circumcision is an irrevocable step into slavery.

More than that, by being circumcised his readers would fall away from the grace of Christ (4). This is strong stuff indeed. But Paul's case is this: in his crucifixion, Jesus has taken the curse of law-breaking onto himself (3:10–14). Even a prominent Jewish Christian like Peter confessed that Israel couldn't keep the law, and it shouldn't be imposed on Gentiles (Acts 15:10).

Paul goes further: to be under the law is to be enslaved to the elemental spirits. The law belongs to the old, evil age from which the Galatians have been freed by Christ (1:4). Paul pictures Christ and the law as two separate spheres of power – one with the power to enslave, the other with the power to set free. Paul stresses that the law is not a pick-and-mix package from which the Galatians can take a few things while maintaining their allegiance to Christ. It is all or nothing.

This is why the obligation to keep the whole law (3b) is tantamount to being 'alienated from Christ' (4) and falling 'away from grace' (4b). Here Paul echoes his argument in 2:17–21. It's important to remember that when Paul speaks of being 'justified by law', he is not suggesting that his rivals taught that we gain entry into God's people by obeying the law; rather, that once we have entered God's people by faith in Jesus (2:15–16), we submit to the law in order to remain in Abraham's family (see 'Stop and think', p. 107).

The key, says Paul, is not law but 'faith' (5a). This verse draws on apocalyptic language and ideas to express both our present experience and our future hope. 'The Spirit' is Paul's shorthand here for the life and power of the new age, the age to come, an age marked by righteousness, that we are able to experience now in the present age because of the death of Jesus. 'Faith' and 'Spirit' here recall Paul's argument in 2:16; 3:1–14, 22–26; 4:6–7 and remind his hearers that they already enjoy the fruits of the age to come through their experience of the Spirit in their lives now in the form of signs and wonders and certainty of their adoption as God's children.

The word 'righteousness' (5) is linked to 'justified' (4) and has both a present and future aspect. Paul is saying that God's future 'rectifying' of all things is pulled back into the present through the cross of Jesus and the outpouring of his Spirit. But we only have a foretaste of it now, hence 'we eagerly await' and 'hope' what is yet to come in all its fullness (5; cf. Romans 8:18–27).

Philippians 3:20 helps us to get a clearer picture of 'the righteousness for which we hope'. There Paul talks of us eagerly awaiting the return of our Saviour from heaven, who will come to set all things right and establish his kingdom on a renewed earth. He will transform us into his glorious likeness and we will rule over creation with him. 'Faith' here is the trust that enables us to look forward to this with eagerness and hope.

And in the light of this, circumcision is an irrelevance. If we are 'in Christ' – used here as almost a geographical term, the sphere we inhabit through faith (6) – then we cannot also be 'in law'. Paul repeats this in even more apocalyptic language in 6:15, as we shall see.

What matters for those in Christ is 'faith working through love' (6b, NRSV). This is the first time the noun 'love' appears. The verb has appeared once before in the letter, in 2:20, a verse which gives us the key to unlock this wonderful phrase.

Galatians 2:20 talks about how Paul lives; 5:6 tells us how we should live. Faith working through love looks like Jesus on the cross. This verse has the twin thrust of reminding us what Jesus did in order that we can be part of God's new people, and calling us to live in the world as Jesus lived. This is the shape of our freedom; faith working through love means that we will be prepared to serve our brothers and sisters – the way of life Paul spells out in 5:13 – 6:10. Notice how strongly Paul words this: 'faith working through love' is the 'only' thing that counts.

Paul intends us to see these verses as a summary of his argument, of the case that he has established through his magnificent Bible study. We can see this because of the clustering of significant words: freedom (1), circumcised (2, 3, 6 – the key work of the law his rivals were imposing on his readers), law (3), justified (4), grace (4), faith (5, 6), the Spirit (5), righteousness (5) and Christ (1, 2, 4, 6).

This theologically rich passage draws the threads of Paul's argument together – and at the same time directs a tough appeal to his readers to choose between Christ and the law, between Paul's gospel and that of his rivals. Having done that, he moves on to a very personal appeal to the children he loves.

Questions

1. What does our freedom in Christ feel like?
2. Paul's rivals wanted the Galatians to be circumcised so that they could swell the membership of their club (see 4:17; 6:12–13). Do we make Christians do equivalent things today, for similar reasons – to show that they belong?
3. Unpack the phrase 'faith working through love'. What does it suggest to you?

5:7–12

Don't lose the plot

Having brought the issue of circumcision to the fore, Paul uses the image of 'cutting' to make a final appeal to the Galatians to reject his rivals.

Paul is bemused and angry. He's expressed his bewilderment at the behaviour of the Galatians before (1:6; 3:1; 4:20). His anger at the effect his  rivals are having among these immature believers has bubbled just below the surface, but here it erupts in indignation and contempt.

Paul often uses the picture of the race to describe the Christian life (see 1 Corinthians 9:24–27, Philippians 3:12–17; 2 Timothy 4:7). And here the metaphor carries on the forward thrust of verses 5–6 with all their eager anticipation of arriving in the kingdom that Jesus is bringing when he returns. But like runners who were doing well, someone has 'cut in' across their path and thrown them into disarray (7 – the NRSV obscures the picture by translating 'cut in' as 'prevent').

Notice that Paul asks them who has done it. We all know the culprits, but Paul is keen for the Galatians to enter into the picture and see the effect his rivals are having on their faith. They are stumbling and possibly straying. The word for 'cut in' has a double meaning, of course, as his rivals are wanting to cut the Galatian men in another way.

The result is serious. They are not obeying the truth. As in 2:5 and 14, so here truth is about community life and not just something we assent to with our minds. Paul's rivals are throwing the whole community off course because they have undermined its confidence in the truth of Paul's gospel.

They are being persuasive, but the rivals are not doing God's work. 'The one who calls you' (8b) recalls 1:6–9 with its solemn warning of judgment on those who pervert the gospel. Paul regularly speaks of God calling people to faith in him (Romans 1:7; 1 Corinthians 1:2 etc). It is his way of showing that God takes the initiative in our relationship with him. It has always been like this (Genesis 12:1–3). He also speaks of God calling him to his role as apostle to the Gentiles (1:15). The contrast, therefore, between the Galatians and their apostle on the one hand, and the rival missionaries on the other, couldn't be clearer.

Indeed, whereas Paul preaches the truth, his rivals' message is like 'yeast' (9). Paul quotes the same proverb here that he uses in 1 Corinthians 5:6, which recalls Jesus' saying about the yeast of the Pharisees (Luke 12:1). He leaves it to his readers to work out how it applies but the implication is clear: if the rivals are allowed to continue preaching their distorted message, they will infect the whole church, throwing it permanently off course and away from the truth.

Paul is confident the Galatians will read it this way (10a). This may be a rhetorical ploy to clinch his argument, as his readers have shown definite signs of being led astray (4:10; 5:3). But his next phrase (10b) leaves nothing to the imagination. It's a warning of judgment on anyone who spreads false teaching in the church. Paul uses the third person singular in this sentence to emphasize that each member of the rival mission team individually will have to face the music for what he is doing. It's a reminder that ultimately we cannot hide in the crowd, but must account for our actions before God.

Then things take a decidedly curious turn. Why would anyone think Paul preaches circumcision (11)? It's possible that the rivals had told the Galatians that this was Paul's practice. Acts 16:1–3 – an episode that we think happens long after Galatians was written – tells of Paul's second journey into the southern part of Galatia where he met and circumcised Timothy from Lystra. Perhaps it was something Paul had done before. Maybe his rivals knew of it and pointed it out to the Galatians. It might be that they did it from the purest of motives, suggesting to these young converts that had Paul stayed around longer, he'd have insisted they all got circumcised, just as they were doing now.

Paul's response to this is twofold. First, he reminds them that he's being persecuted (11) – something his readers already knew (maybe this is why Paul expresses it as a question). His persecutors are almost certainly Jewish opponents who resented his betrayal of Judaism – which is how they view his call and ministry (1:13, 23; 4:29; 6:12, 17). And secondly, he says that if he is 'preaching circumcision', then it would abolish the scandal of the cross (11). This is because Paul would in effect no longer be saying that Christ redeems us from the curse of the law (3:13), because he would no longer view the law as a curse but as a blessing!

Certainly, as a Pharisee, Paul would have preached circumcision (1:13–14). He would have been very zealous for the boundary markers that divided Jew from Gentile. But the cross abolished all that. The word *skandalon* (offence) has a positive connotation in Paul's theology. He explains this clearly in 1 Corinthians 1:18 – 2:5. His argument is simply that the cross overthrows both Greek philosophy and Jewish expectations. The likelihood is that he used similar arguments when preaching in Galatia – otherwise his very abbreviated reference to it here would make no sense. To go back to preaching circumcision would negate the life and world-changing power of the gospel of the faithfulness of Jesus, God's Messiah. It would also make the cross redundant.

So how could he have been preaching circumcision? That would align him with the old age of the law and its works. The thought of this charge seems to make him so angry that his sharp tongue cuts deep into the hearts of his opponents. He calls them 'agitators', people making trouble for the Galatians, stirring up discontent with Paul and his gospel. Then he makes a crude and sarcastic joke at their expense (12) – if they're so keen on cutting, let them castrate themselves, he snarls.

Would his original hearers have laughed or gasped at this point? Perhaps it would have defused the tension and in doing so reinforced the seriousness of Paul's warning. He manages in one phrase to make his rivals look both wrong and foolish.

Questions

1. What are the things that might throw us off course in our Christian lives? What do you think is the 'yeast' affecting the church in our day and culture?
2. Is Paul justified in his use of such savage language against his rivals (12)? Can you envisage using such language in the church today? When? Under what circumstances?
3. The underlying issue here is anger. Paul is furious about these 'agitators' and their influence in Galatia. What role does anger play in the Christian life? (See Ephesians 4:26–27; Colossians 3:8–9; Mark 3:5.)

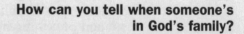

How can you tell when someone's in God's family?

One of the key issues dividing Paul from his rivals was 'how do we know someone is part of God's people'? They agreed on how you start the Christian life: you put your trust in the faithful life and death of Jesus (2:15–16). But they didn't agree on what happened next. Paul's rivals stressed the need for believers to keep the law because that was an objective marker against which to judge a person's faith. If you kept the law and did the works associated with it – especially circumcision, Sabbath, the food laws and holy days – you showed that you had faith.

In some ways, Paul's rivals sounded like James. In his letter, he famously speaks of faith needing to show itself in works (2:14–26); indeed, he seems to contradict Paul by suggesting that Abraham was justified by what he did as much as by his faith in God. However, a careful reading shows that Paul and James agree with each other and neither agreed with what the rival missionaries were preaching in Galatia – whatever they may claim about being endorsed by James.

Nowhere in his letter – or in his message from the Jerusalem council (Acts 15:22–29) – does James suggest that Christians need to submit to the law or do the works of the law in order to demonstrate the validity of their faith in Jesus. All he stresses is that Christians should show the reality of their faith by doing good in the world, something Paul wholeheartedly endorses (2:10; 5:6; 6:10).

For Paul, *living by the Spirit* is evidence of our faith in Jesus (5:16). This is seen in two ways. The first is that we live in a way that builds up the Christian community. His rivals divided people into first- and second-class Christians. Paul argues that all believers are one (3:28) and that through faith in Jesus we are indwelt by the Spirit, who grows in us the qualities we need to create and maintain Christian community. Through the Spirit, we love and encourage, support and help one another (5:22–23; 6:1–2, 9–10). Trusting only in the works of the law, we risk tearing ourselves apart and reaping destruction in our personal lives (5:15, 26; 6:7–8).

The Spirit works in our midst as we walk in step with him (5:25), performing miracles (3:5) and inspiring utterances when the church is gathered for worship (4:6–7). This is evidence that we are part of God's new people.

The second piece of evidence is that we do 'good'. We so often see Paul pitting faith against works, that we fail to notice how much stress Paul puts on Christians being people who do good works (see Ephesians 2:10; Titus 2:11–14; 3:14 – read the whole of Titus in the NRSV and count the number of references to 'good works').

In Galatians, the outcome of being filled with the Spirit is that we do good to everyone, especially those of the family of God (6:9–10). This is how Paul lived – wanting to do good to the poor (2:10), something he did through the collection he raised from the mainly Gentile churches he planted for the poor believers in Judea. For Paul, this too was evidence that people were part of God's family.

5:13–15

Set free to serve

Christ sets us free so that we can become slaves of one another and thus fulfil the heart of the law through living by faith.

Following the slight digression of verses 11–12, Paul now spells out the reasons for what he urged his hearers to do in 5:2–10 and restates the central thesis of the letter – that in Christ we have been set free (5:1). But at first sight what he says is deeply puzzling – we're free, but should live like slaves; we're saved by faith but live to fulfil the law. What's Paul doing?

He first reminds his hearers of their call (1:6, 5:8). In Paul's letters it's always God who calls. It's a reminder that God is their master – not Paul and certainly not his rivals. And we know from 5:1 that it is Christ, God's Son, who won our freedom from the elemental spirits, the law and sin (1:4; 2:19; 3:13; 4:4–5).

Then he tells us that freedom is not to be an excuse for behaving sinfully. The Greek of 13b contains no verb. The NIV supplies 'use', but I think 'receive' would be better, because Paul's emphasis is not on what we do but on the nature of our call by God. He has given us freedom, not so that we can do whatever we like, but so that we may live well.

Paul meets his rivals' obvious objection to his teaching head-on. They would have been arguing that without the law to regulate our behaviour we would be free to indulge our sinful desires, free to do whatever we want . Paul says this isn't the case, because we've been set free from sin and the power of the elemental spirits/principles of the world (which includes the law) in order to be able to live as God wants us to.

And the way God wants us to live is to 'serve one another in love' (13c). From the first half of the verse, we would have expected Paul to say that we should serve God and so resist the temptation to indulge the flesh. But – paving the way for the argument he makes in 5:16 – 6:10 – he urges us to see our freedom as an opportunity to serve one another. He sets up an eternal triangle, with God at the apex and the individual believer and church at the two points on the base. This was probably one of the ways that the early Christians talked about how we should live, because it's also central to the ethical teaching of 1 John (see 1 John 1:5–7; 4:7–12).

Our proper response to God's call and action in setting us free from sin is to become slaves of one another (the verb is stronger than the rather weak 'serve' in the NIV), not slaves of righteousness (as Paul says in Romans 6:18) or slaves of Christ (as he describes himself in 1:10). The reason for this is twofold. First, Paul's emphasis through the letter is not about how individuals are saved, but rather about who constitutes God's people and how they should live in the world. And second, he is about to go on to contrast the works of the flesh with the fruit of the Spirit, where the focus is on our relationships with one another.

In one sense Paul's prescription is not much more palatable than the one offered by his rivals – namely circumcision and keeping the law. Slavery was something people in the Roman Empire wanted to avoid at all costs.

Epictetus, who lived a little later than Paul, argued that people should aspire to be free to choose absolutely how they live, without reference to anyone else. In this he echoed a common Greek philosophical idea.

By contrast, Paul says the way of the Christian is the way of willing slavery. And he argues this because of Jesus. It is his love that is in view at the end of verse 13. It is Jesus who modelled this love in willingly offering his life for ours on the cross (2:20; 5:6). He is the model for our behaviour, says Paul.

In living this way, he goes on to argue, we fulfil the law. Here's another strange thing: Paul's law-free gospel of grace and faith leads to believers fulfilling the law in their lives (14). Why does he say this?

The verb translated 'summed up' (in both the NIV and NRSV) means fulfilled. It is in the perfect tense, the tense used to describe past actions that have effects which continue in the present. So Paul is saying that the whole law has come to fulfilment in a single commandment, the same one that Jesus used in his summary of the law (Mark 12:28–34).

The law has been fulfilled by Jesus and especially by his love (2:20; see 2 Corinthians 3:14–15 – a key text for Paul's understanding of the law). This fulfilment happened both through Jesus' teaching – bringing out the deepest meaning of the whole Old Testament story, including the law – and his death for others which was the perfect embodiment of that meaning. The law is thus fulfilled and reshaped; now when we read it, we see Jesus – hence the perfect tense.

So the verse spells out how believers should behave: we are to behave as Jesus did! We participate in Jesus' fulfilling of the law by our own loving service towards one another. Paul's logic here is parallel to his logic in chapter 3 where he spoke of Christ as Abraham's seed (16) and of us as Abraham's seed by virtue of our faith in Jesus (29). This is what it means to be 'in Christ' (see Romans 8:3–4).

The trouble is that the Galatians are not fulfilling the law in any way at all. They are tearing themselves apart through their rivalry (15). Their bad relationships are clearly a major concern of Paul's because he comes back to them in verse 26, suggesting that the coming discussion of life in the Spirit is intended to deal with precisely this problem. Was the infighting caused by Paul's rivals or did it exist because they arrived? Indeed were they offering the law as a solution to it? After all, many Christians think that a regime of rule-keeping will ensure good order in the church. Galatians 5:7 suggests that life was progressing well until the rivals turned up and confused everyone (an interpretation supported by the parallel situation in Antioch; see 2:11–14).

Questions

1. How can it be called 'freedom' if we have to serve one another?
2. Do a reality check. Test the love levels in your church or fellowship – in prayerful discussion with others, if possible. Be honest: do you 'serve one another in love'?
3. Spend a little time with the commandment 'love your neighbour as yourself'. Be realistic: what does this actually mean in practice?
4. Your church has become divided and the last church meeting was a horrible experience of tense feelings, hostility and harsh words. A bit like the meeting described in Galatians 2:11, in fact. How do we rescue the church so that we don't 'bite and devour one another' completely?

Doctrine and experience

Galatians is almost certainly Paul's earliest letter, written hurriedly in 48 or 49, before he and Barnabas set off for the meeting in Jerusalem reported by Luke in Acts 15. Yet even though it's so early, it contains many of the core doctrines of the Christian faith, indicating that these did not evolve over many decades, but were rather arrived at very quickly in the light of Jesus' ministry, death and resurrection.

In today's church there is a tendency to suggest that doctrine (what we believe) doesn't matter as much as experience. A lot of contemporary Christian worship music focuses on how we feel about God rather than on what we know about God. But for Paul, experience and doctrine were two sides of the same coin. Our experience of God is understood in terms of what we know about him, and our understanding of God is shaped by our experience of him in our lives.

For Paul, the defining experience of his life was meeting Jesus on the Damascus Road. He doesn't go into detail in Galatians, but it is clearly a key moment in his life (see 1:13–16; Acts 9:1–19). And it is hard to overestimate the effect of that experience on Paul.

He had met a Jesus who was alive. So Paul has to change his mind about him: Jesus can't have been the rightly crucified messianic pretender that Paul had thought. If God had raised him from the dead, then his claim to be the bringer of the kingdom, the source of new life, the one who would give the Holy Spirit to his followers and usher in the new age, must be true.

But there was more. If Jesus was the Messiah and he had ended up on a cross, that can't have been an accident. God would not have allowed his plans for his Messiah to be thwarted by chance. So the cross must have been central to Jesus' work as the Messiah, central in the defeat of Israel's enemies and the establishment of God's kingdom – hence Paul's argument in Galatians 2:20, 3:10–14.

And surely there was still more. The glorious appearance of Jesus on the road was very like the glorious appearance of God himself, when he showed himself to people in Old Testament times. What did this tell Paul about who and what Jesus was? Is this why Paul thinks of Jesus as divine? Does it account for Paul's description of

Jesus as *God's Son* (2:20; 4:4 – with its strong hint of pre-existence), as *Lord* (1:3, 6:18) and as the one who jointly with God called Paul to apostleship (1:1).

And finally, why did Jesus say Paul was persecuting him, when he was in fact persecuting the church (see Acts 9:4)? What did this begin to teach Paul about the nature of the church as *the body of Christ* on earth? Does it lie behind Paul's description of believers as God's children, one in Christ, heirs to the promises given to Abraham (3:26–29) ?

This is the Jesus who called Paul to be his messenger to the Gentiles (Acts 9:15). Did this suggest that in Jesus God has broadened the boundaries around his people to encompass people from every nation, tribe and tongue (3:28), so that Israel is now understood to be the people who have faith in Jesus rather than those born in Judea (6:16)? Does that account for his call to be apostle to the Gentiles (1:16)?

Such immediate reactions no doubt fired his period of reflection and early ministry (those years he talks about in 1:17, 21). As Paul read the Old Testament, the law, in the light of his experience of Jesus on the Damascus Road, he came to see how through his life, death and resurrection, Jesus was the fulfilment of the story, the perfect expression of God's saving faithfulness to his people, and the one through whom God's enemies were routed and his kingdom brought to earth.

Although Paul developed his understanding of the Christian faith in the coming years, although he was able in later letters – especially in Romans – to present a more detailed defence of his gospel, nothing he learned later in life suggested that anything he wrote in Galatians needed correction. It is amazing to think that Christian doctrine – our understanding of God, Jesus and his Spirit, the cross and resurrection and the nature of the church as God's people – arrived almost complete.

And this matters because Paul's argument against his rivals is not based on prejudice against them or Paul's desire to exercise power over people he views as his converts. His arguments are based entirely on the truth of the

Christian message, the doctrines that were revealed to Paul in his Damascus Road experience, that were later confirmed and fleshed out by his study of the Old Testament and his conversations with others who followed Jesus.

Right action is based on right thinking, and right thinking is based on right doctrine. This is why Paul's letter has such a large section (most of chapters 3 and 4) devoted to a detailed study of various Bible passages.

It's also why Paul is able to appeal to doctrines that are agreed by everyone. In particular in 2:15–16, Paul is able to appeal to shared understanding of how people start the Christian life – through faith in Jesus – as the basis for what he will go on to argue.

In all our defence of the gospel and our teaching on how to live the Christian life, we need to be sure of our doctrine and base what we say on it. Paul is a model of how to do this.

5:16–21

The role of the Spirit

Having told his readers that they will fulfil the law by living like Jesus, Paul now tells us that this is possible only through co-operating with the Holy Spirit.

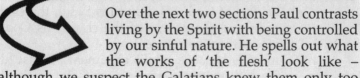

Over the next two sections Paul contrasts living by the Spirit with being controlled by our sinful nature. He spells out what the works of 'the flesh' look like – although we suspect the Galatians knew them only too well – and then outlines the fruit that the Spirit grows in us so that we might live in a different way. As is often the case,

Paul begins by stating his case in headlines (16–17), which he then unpacks over the next few sentences (18–26).

He begins with an emphatic claim to authority – the Greek sentence starts 'But I say ...' – Paul is reminding his readers that he is their founding apostle, the one God used to bring them to faith. They trusted his words then; they should do so now.

It's not the law that will help us to live a good life, but the Spirit. The Spirit is the one who works wonders in their midst (3:5), who has caused them to cry out in worship, '*Abba*, Father ...' (4:6). So, it is the powerful presence of God's Spirit which will give them and us the ability to overcome the flesh – if we 'walk' (indicating that Paul is talking about a way of life, not a one-off action) with him. The NIV is better than the NRSV here, because it captures the idea that *if* we walk by the Spirit, then we *will* avoid gratifying the flesh, as surely as day follows night.

Verse 17 is the theological statement that Paul will unpack in the rest of the chapter. It is a picture of a cosmic struggle. We are fallen, our flesh is sinful, the stuff of our humanity is forged in rebellion against God. The Spirit is the manifestation of God in our midst, poured out into the human sphere as a result of the cross and resurrection of Jesus (3:13–14; 4:6). The struggle is the conflict between the present evil age in which we live and the age to come which has arrived in Christ and is especially made real through the ministry of his Spirit.

This means that the final clause of verse 17 is not a cry of despair. Paul is not lamenting that the flesh is too powerful and he's too weak to resist its desires. Rather, it's a statement of intent. Because we are indwelt by the Spirit, we cannot do certain things, but we can do (in the sense of 'we are allowed to' – the NIV being better than the NRSV here) only those things that the Spirit wants us to. Our freedom in Christ is not absolute. It does not mean that we can do anything we like. Rather, it is the freedom to do what God wants, a freedom that is empowered by the Spirit.

So we're not subject to the law – a set of rules that regulates our behaviour – if we are led by the Spirit (18). This doesn't mean we live in a moral vacuum. Rather, it means we live according to the agenda the Spirit sets for us as individuals and communities. And we live by the power of the Spirit who enables us to live to that agenda rather than engage in the things our sinful natures want. In the war zone that is the world, the Spirit leads us in the way we should go, something the law cannot do because it is not up to the task of overcoming the power of our flesh. There is an implied contrast between the living Spirit who's with us to guide us and the dead letter of the law that inertly sits in judgment of our failures (see 2 Corinthians 3:6).

As if the Galatians – or we for that matter – need it, Paul now outlines the works of the flesh (19–21). There are a number of things to notice about this list.

First, it's a picture of sexual chaos – immorality, promiscuity, debauchery (19b). The law is against these things too – but it's powerless to prevent them. Unrestrained, the flesh leads to marriage breakdown, confused sexual identity and the unravelling of the very relationships that ought to be the building blocks of strong communities. All his hearers would have agreed with this.

Secondly, it's a picture of false religion – idolatry and witchcraft. Our flesh worships what isn't God. We try magic in a bid to manipulate heaven or at least influence our earthly luck. We buy into spiritualities that make us feel good but do nothing to help us live up to our potential as creatures made in the image of God. His hearers would have agreed with this. But his rivals might have felt nervous that he was suggesting that their brand of religion was more about making people feel good about themselves – especially in relation to others who weren't as zealous as they were – than doing God's will.

Thirdly, it's an image of social breakdown. The bulk of this list (especially verse 20) describes things that cause disunity, division and conflict between people. And fourthly (21), it's about loss of control and the chaos and confusion that ensues – of which drunkenness and orgies are all-too graphic examples.

Such behaviour destroys human community – we see it everywhere in the social breakdown of communities in many Western cities and the wars that scar the face of the earth. And it destroys churches. It's what is happening in Galatia as a result of Paul's rivals. Note the strong warning in 21b.

These are not one-off actions or single outbursts of bad behaviour. Paul is talking about a settled way of living (21 – the NIV's 'live like this' is quite right). And he has warned them about behaving this way before (21a), which denies the rumour, no doubt put about by his rivals, that Paul has left them rudderless in a dangerous world by not teaching about the law.

Questions

1. How have you felt the conflict that Paul speaks of in verse 17? Think of practical examples, and share them in discussion with others if possible.
2. How can we avoid reading the list in verses 19–21 and pointing the finger at our neighbours?
3. How do these 'works of the flesh' creep into the life of our churches? How can we best counter the effect that they have?
4. And how do they creep into our lives too? How can we best support and encourage each other in this struggle?

The fruit of the Spirit

Those who are led by the Spirit and seek to model their lives on Jesus find that God grows within them the character traits of their Saviour.

God's remedy to a world tearing itself apart through the sinful behaviour of people and communities is not to bring a big stick and a heavy law book. As Paul has already shown (3:6–22), that doesn't work. Rather, God has dealt with humanity's sin through the cross of Christ and filled those who trust in Jesus with his Spirit, in order that they might have the power to live in the world in a way that reflects his character.

Paul clearly means us to contrast 'the works of the flesh' with 'the fruit of the Spirit' (NRSV is probably right to begin verse 22 with 'by contrast ...', even though the Greek doesn't actually say this). It is important to note that Paul speaks of works (plural, 19) and fruit (singular, 22) and that just as the works of the flesh cause personal and social chaos, so the fruit of the Spirit brings communal harmony and peace.

This list is not about loving, joyful, peaceful individuals in isolation – though, of course, these qualities are personal. Paul's concern is that these qualities are seen in our life together. The works of the flesh divide and corrode community. The fruit of the Spirit builds community. As the Spirit indwells those who join God's people through faith, so he builds our lives together into communities of love, joy, peace, etc.

There is also a contrast between what we do and what God does. In verses 19–21, Paul showed us what we create if we live according to our fallen human nature. In verses 22–23 he shows us what God creates in us by his Spirit.

It's possible that Paul wants us to pay particular attention to the first and last items on the list. 'Love' is the supreme quality of God and the one embodied in Jesus (2:20; 5:13), the basis of our service of one another (see 5:6). 'Self control' as well as being a central virtue in Greek philosophy, is also the polar opposite of the lack of control caused by the works of the flesh outlined in verses 19–21.

In between, Paul identifies qualities being grown in us by the Spirit – some of which were virtues highly prized in the surrounding culture – notably joy and peace. Others – such as gentleness – were qualities associated with slaves and therefore somewhat despised by the chattering classes. Perhaps Paul is making a point by including it! And these qualities are aspects of God's character revealed in the Old Testament and Jesus (especially patience and goodness).

The word translated 'faithfulness' is *pistis*. We have argued that this is the way it should have been rendered at other key points in Galatians (notably 2:16, 20; 3:8, 22; see 'Stop and think', p. 122). The point Paul is making is that just as Jesus was faithful, so we too will be faithful, if we walk by the Spirit – faithful to live out our calling in the world and faithful to our brothers and sisters in helping to build secure and loving Christian communities.

'There is no law against such things' (23b, NRSV) is ironic. Of course there's no law against such qualities. So how can Paul's rivals object to it? This is the outcome they want just as much as Paul does – it's just that their methods (doing the works of the law) will not produce it. Only the Spirit can grow this in us.

Verses 24 and 25 spell this out. We who 'belong to Christ Jesus' have mysteriously participated in his death, his crucifixion; our sinful desires and impulses have been nailed to the cross. Paul is using the same language here of us that he uses of himself in 2:19 and 6:14, though here it is active, something we do, rather than something that is done to us (which is the sense of the other two passages). It is possible that Paul is looking back to his hearers' baptism (as he was in 3:26–29) or at least to the beginning of their Christian lives. What he's saying is this: when we put our trust in Jesus' death on the cross for us, we joined him there, and our old sinful nature, rooted in and wedded to the present evil age, was crucified, so that we could be raised to new life in the age to come, the age of the Spirit. Paul says the same thing in Romans 6:14 and 8:13.

This age has begun now. We are made alive by the Spirit (see 3:2; 4:6–7) – this is what happened when we put our trust in Jesus – so now we should be guided by the Spirit. The word Paul uses here, *stoichōmen*, means to be 'in line with'. It is a playful reference back to the oppressive *stoicheia* that Paul spoke about in 4:3, 9 which ruthlessly kept us in line and imprisoned. Now, says Paul, if 'we walk the line' of the Spirit, we'll know freedom and the wonderful fruit he grows in our lives and community. Paul is also suggesting that the line of the Spirit is better than the line of the law as proposed by his rivals, because it frees us and gives us life, rather than locking us in a prison reeking of death.

This is not theoretical for Paul. The levels of infighting in the Galatian church are such that it is essential his hearers get hold of this. The fires of 'the flesh' have blazed up in the church – precisely as Paul was graphically outlining in verses 19–22, and his rivals are stoking the flames through their obsession with the law. They create envy through pitting one law-keeper against another in a game of competitive holiness. The Spirit, however, sets us free to love one another and joyfully build a community of peace, patience, kindness, generosity, faithfulness, gentleness and self-control.

Questions

1. How may we see the fruit of the Spirit growing in our churches?
2. What do we think it means to be crucified with Christ – in practice?

3. If we're led by the Spirit, what is the place of the Bible in the Christian life?
4. If you're studying with others, why not see if you can present a drama to the rest of the church, illustrating the battle between 'the works of the flesh' and 'the fruit of the Spirit'?

The story of Jesus in Paul's theology

Paul is a storyteller. Everything he writes is based on the great story with which he grew up – the Old Testament story of creation and covenant – interpreted now through the story of Jesus, God's coming king.

This can be seen in Galatians if we look carefully at what Paul says about Jesus and his story. The key is in 3:1, where Paul reminds his readers of their conversion. 'Before your very eyes,' he says, 'Jesus Christ was clearly portrayed as crucified.' That is, he had told them the story of Jesus' life and especially his death on the cross. He tells this story because everyone's salvation depends on it. Galatians 4:4–5 reminds us of the story of Jesus' birth as a Jew, as part of the flow of the great story of faith and redemption that began with Abraham.

In many ways Galatians is about a clash between two stories. The first is told by Paul's rivals and concerns the law. They argue that the Old Testament is the story of the call of Abraham and the giving of the law to his descendants so that they will be faithful to God's expectations of them.

The second is told by Paul and concerns faith. He shows that the unfolding story from Abraham onwards is about faithful living, trusting in the God who calls. He argues that this story reaches its climax in Jesus, the seed of Abraham (3:16), who was faithful to God in all he did. We see this story if we pay close attention to two sections of the letter (2:15–21 and 3:22–26) where Paul talks about the link between the life and faithfulness of Jesus and our faith and consequent lifestyle.

Two key passages tell us the story of Jesus that forms the basis not only for Paul's gospel but also for our living of the Christian life.

Looking at chapter 3 first, we see that Paul uses the story of Jesus' faithfulness to answer Habakkuk's cry about faithless Israel and impending judgment (verse 11 quotes Habakkuk 2:4). How will God rescue his people? Paul's answer echoes God's to Habakkuk – justification doesn't come through the law but through the faithfulness of the righteous one (3:11b says literally 'the righteous *one* by faith will live').

Paul may well intend us to see this as a reference to the Messiah, Jesus, who lived faithfully before God, a theme to which he returns in 3:21–26. Here he contrasts the story of the law with the story of Jesus' faithfulness to God's calling. He is Abraham's seed who, through his obedience, does what the law could never do: secure our forgiveness and place within God's covenant people (justification).

The word faith appears seven times in these verses. In four out of the seven the subject of that faith – the person who has it – is Jesus. In 3:22 we see clearly how our faith is linked to Jesus' faith, for Paul says everything was imprisoned by sin until (literally) 'the promise by the faith of Jesus Christ might be given to the ones believing'. In other words, Paul says that the promise to Abraham comes to fulfilment, not through the law, but through the faithful life and death of Jesus, the benefits of which we enjoy through our faith.

In 3:23 'faith' is literally '*the* faith', indicating that it is the faith just mentioned – that is, the faith of Jesus. Paul says that this faith 'came' and was 'revealed', language that he uses in Galatians only of God (see 1:16) or Jesus (4:4), reinforcing the fact that the faith being talked about here is Jesus' faith not ours. In 3:24 faith is the means by which we are justified – that is our response to Jesus, God's faithful servant.

In 3:25 the faith being referred to is Jesus'. Paul is argu-

ing that we have languished under the law as a hard
taskmaster. But now Jesus has come and freed us from his
control through his faithful life and death (see 3:10).
Finally in 3:26 Paul says that we're no longer under the
law because of our trust in Jesus.

Through this section Paul is arguing that the story that
matters for us is Jesus' story; that is the one we should be
participating in. Indeed, at the climax of this section
(3:26–29) are three references to believers being 'in Christ',
that is that we participate in the life of Christ.

We see this even more clearly in the second passage that
tells us about Jesus' faithfulness (2:15–21). In many ways
this passage is the heart of the letter. Everything else Paul
says hangs on it. And at the heart of this passage is verse
16. The following diagram – which we saw when looking
at these verses in the guide – makes clear the importance
of the story of Jesus for Paul's theology:

  A: Yet we know a person is justified not by works of the
  law
  　B: but through the faith of Jesus (*pisteos Jesu Christou*)
  　　C: And we have come to believe in Christ Jesus
  　B¹: so that we might be justified by the faith of Christ
  　　(*pisteos Christou*)
  A¹: and not by doing the works of the law, because no
  one will be justified by the works of the law.

Our salvation, says Paul, comes from our participation in
the story of Jesus. He lived a life of perfect, faithful obedience. Apart from participation in his story, we are sinners
(17) – whatever our ethnic background – but by becoming
a part of his story through our faith in him, we become
and remain a part of God's covenant people.

This is what Paul means when he talks of being crucified with Christ (20). Here's a crucial reference to the faith
of Jesus. Paul describes the life he lives now in his body in
these words (literally): 'by faith I live that of the Son of
God, the one having loved me and having given himself
over on behalf of me'.

In other words, our ability to live the Christian life depends on our participating in the life of Christ. The gospel is the story of his faithfulness. He obeyed his Father perfectly and so enjoys the inheritance promised to Abraham. We share that by trusting him. The gospel is the power of God because it is the powerful story of the one faithful life ever lived, the story of Jesus.

6:1–5

Looking out for each other

Having outlined how walking with the Spirit is the key to Christian lifestyle, Paul now earths it in the real lives of Christian communities.

All through Galatians Paul has been stressing that the Christian life is lived in community; it is not a solo venture. But how do we do it? Here Paul lays down some simple but profound guidelines for living together in the Spirit. In short, the church should be a place of mutual accountability and support, a place where individuals, aware of their strengths and weaknesses, play their part in the life of the church.

Family is Paul's favourite picture for the church. He uses the language of family in all his letters, especially referring to fellow believers as brothers and sisters (see for instance, Romans 16:1–20; 1 Corinthians 8:8–13). So here, he opens this brief list of instructions by addressing his hearers as 'brothers' (which includes the sisters as well – but the NRSV rendering of 'friends' fails to capture this family language).

The church ought to be a place of mutual support and

encouragement in contrast to the picture of what might have been happening in the Galatian congregations in 5:15 and 26. It is possible that there is a hint here of Paul saying that those who agree with him should gently seek to persuade those who don't to change their minds and come back into fellowship – though we need to balance this with his words in 4:30.

Certainly this applies more generally to lifestyle issues in the church – the 'sin' (1) is visible in the church. Despite 5:16, Paul knows that believers will sin – the word he uses is 'transgression' which has to do with breaking the law – but that they won't settle into a lifestyle of sin (of the kind he condemns in 5:21). Indeed, the word he uses here – which also means 'false step', 'fall beside' – may be a deliberate contrast to 'walking the line' of the Spirit (5:25).

The transgressor is contrasted with those who are spiritual – the Greek word is plural indicating that what is about to be recommended is a team activity, not a solo venture. The spiritual are those whose lives are being shaped by the Holy Spirit (as the NRSV makes clear). The activity of restoration spelled out here is neighbour-love in action (5:14) – the essence of the law fulfilled in us who believe in Jesus. This could explain why Paul uses the more specific word 'transgression' rather than the general word for sin.

The aim is that the spiritual 'restore' the 'transgressor', bring him or her back into the fold, into an experience of the Spirit in their life. They are to do this gently – the same word used in the fruit list of 5:22 – not in a holier-than-thou frame of mind. More importantly, they need to watch out. Towards the end of verse 1 Paul switches to a second person *singular* verb – he is speaking to each individual who might be involved in such restoration: watch out that you don't fall into temptation! What Paul probably has in mind is that 'the spiritual' might be tempted to feel superior to the sinner and so trip over their egos.

This is burden-bearing in action (2). It is how 5:13 will be worked out practically in the community of believers. More than that, it is to live in conscious imitation of Jesus.

The phrase 'fulfil the law of Christ' is an odd one in a letter that has pitted law against faith. But the clue to its meaning is in 5:14, where we read that Christ fulfilled the law (specifically Leviticus 19:18) through his demonstration of self-giving love on the cross (1:4; 2:20). In our behaviour towards one another – especially towards those who are struggling and even sinning – we are to re-enact the event through which Jesus fulfilled the law, namely his self-sacrifice.

The structure of the sentence (2) is the same as 5:16 – a present imperative (that is a verb of command) followed by a future indicative (a verb that says how things will be). That is to say, if we obey a command to live a certain way, predictable consequences will follow. In this case, if we gently seek to restore a wayward brother or sister, we will certainly be fulfilling the law of Christ. There is also an irony here: Paul is contrasting the law of Christ – seen in love and self-sacrifice and resulting in freedom – with the works of the law preached by his rivals which lead to slavery.

Paul elaborates on the need to watch ourselves (3–5). The temptation is that we'll compare ourselves with our brothers and sisters and assume we're doing better than they are (3; see 2 Corinthians 13:5 – a close parallel – and Romans 12:3; 1 Corinthians 11:28). The problem is that if we compare ourselves to one another, it's easy to think that we amount to something – especially if we're selective about whom we compare ourselves to! In doing this, we show that we are in fact nothing.

So, who should we compare ourselves to? Jesus. It's strange in a letter that plays down the works of the law to find the word 'work' (singular) here (4 – 'actions' in the NIV). But the 'work' in view is that of living like Jesus did, doing the kinds of things he would have done (5:6). Paul has more than half an eye on the day of judgment, when we will have to account for our work (see 'Stop and think', p. 107). The clue to that is that he uses the word *kauchēma*, which means 'boasting' and is a word that Paul almost exclusively uses to speak of his attitude to the day of judgment (Romans 15:17; 1 Corinthians 9:16; 2 Corinthians 1:12–14; Philippians 2:16). *Kauchēma* does not mean being big-headed, as boasting often does in English. Rather, it means taking a rightful pride in what we have achieved in the grace God has given us.

This is a burden we carry alone (5). Our brothers and sisters can't carry it for us (2). So we must always be comparing ourselves not to one another – which is a recipe for rivalry or complacency – but to Jesus (his fulfilling of the law through loving self-sacrifice, 2). If we do that, and commit ourselves to living in the light of that comparison, we'll have something to boast about on the day of judgment.

Questions

1. How can we help a brother or sister who's obviously struggling in their Christian life, without coming across as busybodies?
2. How can we help one another to model our lives on Jesus' life?
3. If we shouldn't compare ourselves to one another, what place do heroes play in the Christian life?
4. How do you feel about the day of judgment? Do you think that you will have anything to boast about? (Don't forget the list of heroic qualities that God values in 5:22.)

Sowing and reaping

What we do in this life matters, not just to our brothers and sisters in the church, but also to God – so let's live well!

Some have suggested that 6:1–10 is a random gathering of titbits of good advice. But this isn't the case at all. Paul is keen to spell out how we should live together as Christians in the light of what he has said in the letter and of God's coming judgment – a theme in verses 3–5 and 7–8.

It is therefore vital that Christians know what they're supposed to believe and how those beliefs apply to our daily lives in the world as well as in the church (see 'Stop and think', p. 107 and 132). This could be why Paul interrupts his teaching about examining ourselves with a reference to teachers and teaching (6).

Our teachers will keep us up to the mark in our efforts to live as Jesus did. And because of this we should ensure they are rewarded – the phrase 'all good things' (6b) is a lovely description of being generous and open-hearted. This suggests that even at this early stage in the church's development – probably only fifteen years or so after Jesus' death and resurrection – some people already earned all or part of their living by teaching the Christian faith. All of us have the Holy Spirit (1) and so can teach one another (see Colossians 3:16). But we all need the systematic teaching of Christian truth and help with applying it to our lives, which comes from those with the gifting and the time to devote to it.

Having paused to make that point, Paul returns to the theme of living well in the light of the coming judgment.

The transition between verses 6 and 7 seems abrupt and awkward. It's possible that Paul suddenly thinks of something else he wants to say about judgment after his secretary has committed his words about teachers to the parchment. Certainly 7b follows smoothly on from verse 5. So it's possible that Paul wanted to drive home the point about us being accountable for how we have lived.

He does so by using by an agricultural metaphor. The load we carry on judgment day (5) will be the harvest we have sown in this life. The fact that he introduces it with the stern word about God not being mocked suggests that Paul has his rivals in his sights once again. But we mustn't let that prevent us from applying these words to ourselves as well.

Paul's rivals are certainly 'sowing to the flesh' – literally, in demanding circumcision of men, and metaphorically, in keeping people stuck in the present age of the law, rather than allowing them to experience properly the freedom of the new age of the Spirit. They are 'mocking God' by the way in which they play down the cross of Jesus through their insistence that the Galatians do the works of the law.

But Paul's main point here is broader. It's that each of us needs to be sure where our priorities lie. He has in mind proverbial sayings such as Proverbs 22:8 and Job 4:8. Circumcision for these Gentile believers would certainly be sowing to the flesh (8a), but so is trusting in money or social status or political power. Sowing to the flesh is trusting in and living for the things of this world, this present evil age.

Sowing to the Spirit (8b), by contrast, is placing one's hope in the world to come, manifested in Jesus, made certain through his cross, brought to us by the Spirit and coming fully when Jesus returns (though this is a theme not much stressed in Galatians).

In a very real sense 6:8 sums up the whole letter. Paul is urging us not to put our trust in anything human that belongs to this present age. Rather, we should put our trust in the God who is bringing in the age to come, through the cross of his Son, in the power of his Spirit. All this is more than hinted at in the use of the phrase 'eternal life'. Paul doesn't use this phrase much, but when he does, he uses it with the force of its literal meaning – 'the life of the coming ages' – and its use in Jewish apocalyptic writings to denote the life of the coming age of God's kingdom.

In the light of this, how we live in the present matters. We're in the middle of a story. Twice in 6:9–10 Paul uses the word *kairos* meaning 'time', referring first to the future (9 – the harvest time of God's judgment) and then to the present (10 – the time of opportunity we have now, to live for Christ). It's easy to lose heart in the midst of the struggle to keep in step with the Spirit (9a), but let's persist in doing good, he says (9a), because the time is coming when we'll reap the harvest we want if we don't lose heart. There's a real urgency in these verses. The sowing will end and the reaping begin before we know it – so let's have something worth reaping. What will that be? The fruit of doing good works here and now.

Paul is saying here (as he does in 1 Corinthians 15:58) that what we do in this life matters. So we should seize every opportunity to do good (10a). The word translated 'opportunity' is that word *kairos* again. Paul means that these opportunities to do good works for people are significant times in our lives through which we sow to the Spirit. There's a random generosity about how Christians should live, says Paul; we do good works to anyone and everyone as the opportunity arises – so let's be on the lookout for them. But there's also a settled determination to do good to one another, our brothers and sisters.

Questions

1. In what ways might we sow to the flesh in our lives and churches?
2. What good things should we be sharing with all those who teach us the Christian faith?
3. How can we help one another seize opportunities to do good to those around us?

4. Individually we seem so insignificant. What difference do our good works make in the world? How can they affect global realities on planet earth? Why should we bother?

Our identity in Christ

Paul's letter to the Galatians raises crucial questions about the relationship of Christians to the culture they live in; questions that are as pertinent today as they were in Paul's day. These are questions that have to do with our identity – both personally and as members of a community or citizens of a nation.

It is possible that one of the reasons why the rival missionaries' message fell on fertile soil in Galatia is that it offered the new converts a secure identity in a society where who you were and where you fitted in the pecking order was very important. It also explains why Paul focuses so much on issues of identity, both personal and communal, in his outline of the gospel.

Like most of the Roman Empire, first-century Galatia was a melting pot of religious and philosophical ideas. But we mustn't make the mistake of thinking that it was a liberal democracy like the modern Western world, where people were entirely free to choose a faith from a supermarket of religious options on offer. Rather, people were expected – indeed obliged – to toe the civic line on religion.

In particular, everyone was expected to join in the public veneration of the emperor and his family. On certain days through the year, every household was obliged to offer sacrifices to the emperor and prayers for him and his family. The so-called 'imperial cult' was the fastest growing religion in the first century and was particularly popular at the eastern end of the Empire. In the cities of Galatia, teeming with Roman citizens and those aspiring to make something of themselves in the Empire, the cult was big business. Archaeologists have found large temple sites in Pisidian Antioch, Iconium and Lystra – the very cities Luke tells us Paul visited on his early travels in Galatia (Acts 13 – 14).

Participation in the cult was a key means of generating social cohesion and a common identity among all citizens of the Empire. But some were exempt from the obligation. Rome granted to Jews the status of *religio licita* ('permitted religion'), which meant that they didn't have to offer sacrifices, though they did have to pray for the emperor. The tell-tale sign that a man was Jewish was circumcision – something looked upon with much scorn by Greco-Roman culture – and observance of the dietary laws and the Sabbath.

It is possible that, in pressing their case for Gentile converts to observe the works of the law, the rival missionaries were offering them a way out of a potential problem. As converts to a faith that proclaimed one Lord (Jesus) and denied the claims of any other god – whether in heaven or on earth (1 Corinthians 8:4–6) – the Gentile Galatians could well have found themselves on the receiving end of persecution by their neighbours and the authorities for not joining in the obligatory imperial cult. The rival missionaries' message of following Jesus and doing the works of the law offered a way out: they would be Christians but they would appear Jewish to their neighbours, legitimately exempted from cult obligations because Judaism was a *religio licita*.

This is clearly hinted at Galatians 6:12–13, where some of the language Paul uses is legal terminology, suggesting that his opponents were offering the Galatians a face-saving way of avoiding being persecuted for the cross of Christ.

Of course, for Paul such a course of action was abhorrent. The freedom Christ brings is freedom from works of the law and bondage to cultural norms and idolatrous religion. In 4:1–11 he demonstrates how the elemental spirits enslave, but the Holy Spirit sets us free. More than that, he does so by giving us a new identity: we are sons of God who cry '*Abba*, Father ...' We are heirs of the kingdom of the true king (4:6–7). Our allegiance is, therefore, not to Caesar or to any other false god, but to Jesus as Lord and Saviour.

Such an identity comes at a price, however: the risk of persecution by the dethroned gods which Paul says is his experience and, by implication, will be the experience of the Galatians if they hold firm (6:12–14).

Paul stresses that our identity is centred on Jesus: we have been crucified with him and the life we now live in the world – the world of politics and consuming, working and playing – we now live through the faithfulness of Jesus (2:20). The world has been crucified to me and I to the world – indicating that its values and ways of creating identity no longer have any hold over me (6:14).

6:11–18

In the end it's about the cross and the new creation

Seizing the pen to write his final greetings, Paul can't help but underline the key themes of the letter and appeal once more to his readers to keep the faith.

With pen in hand Paul underlines the key themes of the letter. He wants his readers to see how important this is because he writes it in big letters (11a). But just as at the start of the letter, there's no time for greetings, as he'd normally write. Rather, he offers a careful summary of his entire argument. It's a sign of how urgent Paul feels this is. But it's also an indication of just how strained the relationship is between Paul and these churches.

He begins (12–13) by attacking his opponents one final time over the issue of circumcision (see 5:2–3). His rivals are trying to 'compel' them to submit to it ('compel' is the same verb as in 2:3–4, where the false brothers wanted Titus circumcised, but the Jerusalem leaders wouldn't compel it, 14).

Why did they want this? Partly because they want the Gentile converts to keep the law (just as Paul has been arguing in chapters 3 – 4), but mainly so that they won't be persecuted. How come? It is likely that militant Jews – Pharisees and Zealots – were stirring up trouble for Christians in Jerusalem and Judea over their contact with Gentiles. In order to ease the pressure, some Jewish Christians could well have been urging Gentile converts to get circumcised – become fully 'Jewish' though still remain followers of Jesus – and so reduce the threat to Jewish Christian communities in Judea.

Paul had certainly persecuted Christians before his call (1:13). And it's possible that this had been part of his motive for this – though in those early days there were few Gentile converts. It's also possible that his rivals thought that Paul still preached circumcision for the same reason (5:11). Paul didn't, of course – of which more in a moment.

So, he's suggesting that his rivals are urging the Galatians to get circumcised in order to make their own lives easier (12b). Just for good measure, he adds that the circumcised – by which he means all Jews – can't keep the law (13), that this ritual act doesn't help anyone live the kind of life the law urges on us. Peter will agree with this in his statement at the Jerusalem meeting (Acts 15:10–11). Notice how similar his statement is to Galatians 2:15–16, suggesting that it comes after his face-off at Antioch, from which he's learned a crucial lesson! Paul is accusing his rivals of hypocrisy – they compel circumcision on others but don't keep the law themselves (which is exactly what he accused Peter of in 2:14).

Their only reason for compelling Gentiles to get circumcised is so that they might boast about their 'flesh' (13c) – literally (almost counting scalps!) and metaphorically, where 'flesh' is contrasted with 'Spirit'. The word 'flesh' appears in both 12 and 13: Paul wants to stress that his rivals' whole scheme is based on the flesh as opposed to the Spirit, law as opposed to grace (though the latter term does not appear here).

Their boasting could well be to non-Christian Jews – a way of showing how they are being more faithful to their ancestral traditions (by bringing in the Gentiles in the proper way) than the Zealots are.

Talk of boasting leads Paul to remind them that he only boasts about the cross (14a). The irony here is that the cross is *God's* work, the place where all human pride and boasting is shattered. Boasting in the cross is to admit that we are totally dependent on God's grace for our place in God's people. Paul makes the same point in more detail in 1 Corinthians 1:18 – 2:5.

He then graphically describes the outcome of the cross – *my* crucifixion (14b). Paul's old identity as a zealous, law-keeping, Christian-persecuting Pharisee has gone. His new identity is as a follower of Jesus, a participator in his death and resurrection (see 2:19–20).

The old things that once mattered – ethnic markers, works of the law that separated Jew from Gentile – don't matter any more (15). If 3:28 is true, then circumcision is a total irrelevance. Paul's sentence is wonderfully broken. What he writes is literally: 'Neither circumcision is anything nor uncircumcision but new creation.' It's very similar to 2 Corinthians 5:17 where what he writes literally means: 'so if anyone in Christ, new creation. Everything old has passed away. See everything has become new.' The gospel, in short, is about a new world made by God. It is the fulfilment of Isaiah 65:17 and is fundamental to Paul's understanding of what God has achieved through Jesus. It's not just about individual salvation; it's all about the re-creation of the cosmos of which we're an important part.

This is the essence of Paul's apocalyptic gospel as presented in Galatians. It opens with the assertion that Jesus rescued us from the present evil age (1:4) and closes with this ringing declaration that the new creation has come. Paul's gospel is all about this, whereas the teaching of his rivals is rooted in the present age of sin, division and rebellion.

Having cursed those who oppose his gospel (1:8–9), he now blesses those who follow it (16b). What is the 'rule' he has in mind? It's keeping in step with the Spirit (16a). See 5:25, where Paul uses the same verb (in the future tense, as he does here), indicating that this new creation rule breaks the grip of the old rules. Such people, he says, will know mercy and peace.

And who are these people? What does 'Israel of God' refer to here? The answer hinges on how we interpret *kai* ('and') that links the two phrases in 16b. Does it mean 'and' implying blessing on two distinct groups, Christians and Israel? Or does it mean 'even/that is', implying that there is one group in view? It is hard to decide for sure. But the flow of the argument of Galatians suggests that Paul is saying that all who keep the rule outlined in this letter are the 'Israel of God' upon whom he pronounces a special singular blessing.

After all, Paul describes the Gentile Galatian believers as the children of Abraham (3:6–9), heirs to the promise (3:29), Sarah's children and heirs of Isaac's promise (4:28, 31). They are the ones who fulfil the law (5:14; 6:2). They are these things because of their faith in Jesus, the seed of Abraham (3:16). The Israel of God (6:16) are those who are in Christ (3:26–29), the new community of God's people gathered around Jesus and led by his Spirit, made up of both Jews and Gentiles.

Paul's final plea for a hearing and for his hearers to reject his rivals is because of his scars (17). He has been persecuted for his message and he interprets these beatings in terms of Christ. He speaks in a similar way in 2 Corinthians 4:10; 6:4–5; 11:23–27. His battle-scars speak of his integrity and his faithfulness to the gospel – as they had done when he first preached it to them (4:13–14). These marks in a Mediterranean slave culture would also have been evidence that Paul was a slave of Jesus (1:10).

His deep desire is that his hearers would know the grace of Christ (18), the grace that he has outlined at length in this impassioned and wonderful letter.

Questions

1. Look back over the whole letter. What single thing have you learned from your study of Galatians that has made a difference to the way you live your Christian life? Share your reactions with others if you are studying as a group.
2. How have you experienced the new creation Paul speaks of?
3. What does it mean to 'boast in the cross of our Lord Jesus Christ'? Remember that the cross was the most shameful form of execution imaginable, bringing its awful shame on the victim's family and friends.
4. How should we preach the gospel to Jewish people?

Further reading

There's a wealth of good reading on Galatians; here's a selection of books I've found invaluable.

Commentaries (in order of usefulness)

Richard B. Hays, *Galatians* (New Interpreters Bible volume 11, Abingdon Press, 2000) – a lucid, masterly commentary only available in a rather expensive large volume. It's the one I turn to first.

Tom Wright, *Paul for Everyone: Galatians and Thessalonians* (SPCK, 2002) – an excellent popular commentary by a leading New Testament scholar.

Walter Hansen, *Galatians* (IVP, 1994) – a solid and reliable guide to the letter for preachers and home group leaders.

Richard Longenecker, *Galatians* (Word Biblical Commentary, Nelson, 1990) – an exhaustive treatment, well informed but requires a working knowledge of Greek to get the best from it.

John Stott, *The Message of Galatians*, The Bible Speaks Today (IVP, 1968) – a classic and scholarly reading of Galatians, accessible to the lay person.

Background books

All of these are quite demanding but repay careful reading.

N. T. Wright (the same 'Tom Wright' as above), *Paul: Fresh Perspectives* (SPCK, 2005) – an excellent overview of the current debate about Paul and his theology by a master scholar and communicator.

Bruce W. Longenecker, *The Triumph of Abraham's God: The Transformation of Identity in Galatians* (T. & T. Clark, 1998) – a wonderful reading of Galatians in the light of modern questions about identity, especially the identity of

God's people in a changing world.

J. Louis Martyn, *Theological Issues in the Letters of Paul* (T. & T. Clark, 1997) – mainly devoted to Galatians, Martyn particularly focuses on the apocalyptic nature of Paul's gospel.

John Barclay, *Obeying the Truth: A Study of Paul's Ethics in Galatians* (T. & T. Clark, 1988) – an excellent study of the role of the Holy Spirit in forming Christian character and community cohesion.